The
Anti-Racist
Cookbook

The
Anti-Racist
Cookbook

A Recipe Guide for Conversations About Race That Goes Beyond Covered Dishes and "Kum-Bah-Ya"

Robin Parker
Pamela Smith Chambers

CRANDALL,
DOSTIE &
DOUGLASS
BOOKS, INC.

Roselle, NJ

Published by Crandall, Dostie & Douglass Books, Inc.
245 West 4th Avenue
Roselle, NJ 07203-1135

(908) 241-5439
www.CDDbooks.com

Edited by Lisa Purcell
Cover and Interior Design by Nancy J. Hajeski

First printing 2005

ISBN: 0-9719017-6-7

Library of Congress Control Number: 2005920695

ATTENTION CORPORATIONS, UNIVERSITIES, COLLEGES, AND PROFESSIONAL ORGANIZATIONS: Quantity discounts are available on bulk purchases of this book for educational, gift purposes, or as premiums for increasing magazine subscriptions or renewals. Special books or book excerpts can also be created to fit specific needs. For information, please contact the publisher.

Notice: The information in this book is true and complete to the best of our knowledge. It is offered without guarantee on the part of the authors or Crandall, Dostie & Douglass Books, Inc. The authors and Crandall, Dostie & Douglass Books, Inc. disclaim all liability in connection with the use of this book.

PUFFIN FOUNDATION LTD.
"...continuing the dialogue between art and the lives of ordinary people."

Funding for this book has been made possible by the Puffin Foundation.

10 9 8 7 6 5 4 3 2 1

• • • • • • • • • • • • • • • • • • •

To our friend and colleague, Nancy Mamis-King,
whose inspiration and fiery spirit guided us throughout
the writing of this book. And to Eric Johnson,
whose memory has given us strength in our work.

To my parents, Robert H. Parker and Wylma M. Parker

—Robin

To my parents, Walter H. Smith and Virginia Smith

—Pamela

• • • • • • • • • • • • • • • • • •

Thanks to our Benefactors

● ●

The following persons helped support the publication of this book through generous financial contributions:

David Arnold

Birgit Ayrey

Marty Battista

Better Beginnings
    Child Development Center

Marilyn Bonner

William A. Borden and
    Terri Borden

Gary Carswell

Barbara F. Flythe

James W. Glassen, Esq.

Gloucester City Human
    Relations Committee

Larry James

William Knight

Linda Konrad-Byers

Lynne C. Marysdaughter

Howard A. McGinn

Yumiko Mishima

Tywana and Drew Smith

Dorothy J. Stewart

Rosalie Stutz

Jane M. Sweeney

Marietta Taylor

Hing and Mary P. Tong
    Foundation

Debbie and Gary Vermaat

Stuart Watts

Gary and Lydia Williams

Michele A. Woods and
    Aubrey J. Kauffman

A special contribution toward the publication of *The Anti-Racist Cookbook* was made in memory of the late Ruth Tipton by her nephew, who believes that she had the potential to be transformed by this book.

Contents

• •

Introduction

• •

*A single conversation across the table with
a wise person is worth a month's study of books.*
—Proverb

Why We Have Written This Book

When we ask, "Should we talk about race in the United States?" the response is usually, "Let's talk about something else!" It is strange that while race has been called "the great American obsession," it is not an obsession most people are willing to discuss. No doubt, the history of racial attitudes and discrimination often leaves us feeling guilty or humiliated: slave codes, "black codes," and Jim Crow laws codified racial inequities through the 1960s. And if racial unrest, which continues even into the twenty-first century, seems an impossible place to begin a dialogue, the topic of slavery will certainly end one.

The economic consequences of race also leave us with few comfortable starting places for discussion. How do we muster the courage to peer over the dinner table to discuss why an African American or Latino/a will generally earn less money than his or her white counterpart (although they both have the same qualifications and do the same job)? The impossibility of the conversation explains not only why we don't have the racial conversation, but also why we usually don't have different-race friends at the table at all. Although cultural diversity in the United States is growing, most of us choose to form our intimate associations (best friend, golf buddy, partner or spouse) with persons who have the same racial backgrounds as we do.

With so much "happening" around race, yet so little spoken about race, the topic takes on a forbidden air. Our worst fear is that confronting racial issues will lead us to violence like that which followed the verdict in the "Rodney King case." (That 1992 Los Angeles race riot was the deadliest and most destructive in U.S. history. Fifty-two people died and property valued at one billion dollars was destroyed.) Our habit is usually to avoid the bogeyman of race and hope that he will disappear: "Let's talk about how much we have in common, not our differences!" Lurking under this social deep freeze of fear and avoidance is the uneasy notion that we can and should do something to discuss—and begin to solve—the issue of race, but how to do so remains elusive.

The Anti-Racist Cookbook is our answer to the question, "Why can't we all just get along?" We can! We just need some basic recipes to help us. In the style of all cookbooks, *The Anti-Racist Cookbook* offers a list of ingredients and preparations that will enable you to feed yourself well, not with food, but with knowledge, ideas, and discussion strategies that can improve the places where you live, work, and study. So, take this book with you, dog-ear the pages, discuss the contents over lunch, dribble coffee on the cover, modify the suggestions so that they fit your palate, allow yourself to make mistakes along the way! The magic of this cookbook is in the way it encourages us to fill up with the rich delicacies of trust, candor, and community. Bland recipes for mere political correctness are not on the menu.

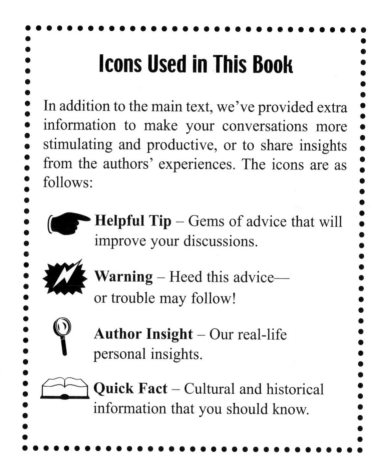

Icons Used in This Book

In addition to the main text, we've provided extra information to make your conversations more stimulating and productive, or to share insights from the authors' experiences. The icons are as follows:

Helpful Tip – Gems of advice that will improve your discussions.

Warning – Heed this advice— or trouble may follow!

Author Insight – Our real-life personal insights.

Quick Fact – Cultural and historical information that you should know.

Who This Book Is For

The Anti-Racist Cookbook is an easy-to-use discussion guide to race issues for adults and young adults. We designed the book for persons interested in improving their personal, community, and work lives through discussion and self-reflection. Some of the groups and individuals who can benefit from the *Cookbook* are:

- Individuals seeking personal growth
- Students
- Educators
- Community groups
- Families
- Trainers
- Social justice advocates
- Work groups
- Faith-based organizations

What You Can Accomplish by Talking About Race

A discussion guide like *The Anti-Racist Cookbook* invites the question, "What difference will talking make?" The answer may surprise you. Often, people think that talking is inaction; no matter how useful, discussions are given low priority. Yet, discussion has a special power that is too often overlooked: the ability to change attitudes. Great historical events happened not simply because people made changes in their lives or institutions, but because they were first *persuaded* to make change. The engine of discussion drives changes in personal beliefs.

The American Revolution is a ready example. The Boston Massacre, the Boston Tea Party, and the Stamp Act are often cited as three of the most important events that led to the American Revolution. Without more, however, those events would not have rallied people to action. Most American colonists were content with British rule. So, a few patriots used the power of public discourse to change history. Through discussions inspired by articles, sermons, announcements, proclamations, and town meetings, patriots persuaded the colonists that the Boston Massacre, the Boston Tea Party, and the Stamp Act happened because Great Britain was a despotic ruler. Those discussions convinced the colonists to embrace independence.

Your discussions about race have the power to change attitudes—yours and your fellow participants'—as well. As you use this book, you can expect these changes to happen:

- You will better understand your own cultural background.
- You will learn how your cultural background influences your perception of others.
- You will build a shared vision of how you can create a truly inclusive and respectful sense of community with other persons, especially those whose backgrounds are different from your own.
- Your understanding about race and other cultural differences will deepen.
- You will build allies in your efforts to promote fairness for others in their communities and workplaces.

How We Approach Cross-Race Conversations

Both of us have years of experience talking about race while conducting diversity training for organizations and individuals, or facilitating small-group discussions in communities. In *The Anti-Racist Cookbook*, we set forth our approaches so that you can understand and adopt them as your own. They have produced wonderful results for us.

Anti-Racism Is Key

The Anti-Racist Cookbook uses an anti-racism approach to cross-cultural communication. Approaches to diversity can take many forms. They include "equal employment opportunity" approaches that seek to ensure compliance with anti-discrimination laws, and "cultural competence" approaches that seek to teach the cultural mores of religious, ethnic, and racial groups. Although these approaches have merit, they fall short because they overemphasize how people are the same or fail to address power imbalances among various groups.

A company that is seeking to deter sexual harassment in the workplace, for example, will educate employees about state and federal laws that prohibit discrimination, and how sexual harassment, a form of discrimination carried out primarily against women, can arise on the job. The emphasis in training the employees is usually to convince them that women—just like men—deserve a fair opportunity. Treating women just like men is usually touted as the key to solving the problem.

Although everyone would agree that women should be treated fairly, the implication that women are *just like* men is not correct. Because talking about the historical antecedents of sexism is usually too daunting for workplace training, it becomes easier to advise the staff to adopt a bland, "safe," way of interacting with everyone so that gender differences are treated as if they don't exist.

Women, however, *are* often "different." For example, because women are more likely to be subject to sexual harassment than men, they tend to be more aware of such harassment when it arises. Also, women are frequently in the position of taking primary responsibility for caring for their children while balancing work demands. They also tend to use more relational communication styles and work more collaboratively. These things are part of many women's experiences in the workplace. But because companies teach their employees that everyone should be treated "the same," little attention is paid to the ways women should be treated so that they have a *welcoming* workplace environment, one that would truly enhance productivity. It seems too complicated and risky to treat everyone fairly while also recognizing and addressing their differences, many of which are driven by gender experiences.

The anti-racism approach to diversity can be used to look at any form of oppression such as sexism, anti-Semitism, or homophobia. In *The Anti-Racist Cookbook* we look at racism. This approach uses the following principles:

WE NEED TO LOOK AT RACIAL DIFFERENCES FIRST, NOT THE WAYS WE ARE THE SAME.

We're often in a hurry to talk about the things we have in common. It seems like a safe way to build a sense of community. But for people of color, who find themselves being treated differently every day because of race or ethnicity, talking about our commonalities fails to talk about much of their lives. Talking about our commonalities also ignores the fact that white people are treated

Author's Insight – Robin
DIFFERENCES ARE IMPORTANT

When I conduct a diversity training, a participant (usually white) often asks, "Why do we need to concentrate on racial differences so much? Why can't I just be Steve and everyone else can just be Bob and Carol and Lydia?" Usually a person of color will give the answer: "I can't just be Carol! Being a person of color means my life is shaped by race every day. How people treat me, what I have to teach my children, where I feel welcomed are all shaped by my racial background and the way people see me as 'different.'"

differently than people of color. The experience of walking through life without being the target of racial prejudice is not a norm; it is actually a unique experience that only certain people share. The anti-racism approach emphasizes the need to balance our knowledge of racial differences with human universals. In that way, the full experience of white people and people of color is honored.

EVERYONE HAS PREJUDICES.

We've been taught that only bad people have prejudices. Actually, we all have them. Stereotyped images on television (Remember Tonto, Amos and Andy, the Frito Bandito, and the Taco Bell Chihuahua?), racial jokes from friends and family, and living in culturally homogenous neighborhoods make developing prejudices about others unavoidable. The anti-racism approach emphasizes the need to drop the pretense of non-prejudice and acknowledge our personal need to unearth our own prejudices so that we can address them. If we do so, we can develop deep, meaningful relationships with others.

RACISM NEGATIVELY AFFECTS EVERYONE.

Racism is usually seen as a problem for persons of color. In reality, it is a problem for white people as well. Racism keeps white people fearful of persons of color, stifles the building of deep relationships, keeps stereotypical thinking in place, and promotes an underclass of people. The anti-racism approach emphasizes that racism is a problem that we must solve together because white people are equal stakeholders in building a just society.

WE MUST TALK ABOUT INSTITUTIONAL POWER TO ADDRESS RACISM.

Racism is racial discrimination coupled with societal power. Racial discrimination is bad, but distinct from racism, it is not systemic: it flows only from discreet individuals and therefore is less likely to hurt others over the course of their lives. Racism is especially damaging, however, because it flows from society at large (especially institutions like schools, the courts, and businesses), which affects the ability of persons to reach their full potential. The anti-racism approach emphasizes that if we want to make real change, we must talk about racism and learn how even well-meaning individuals inadvertently keep racism alive.

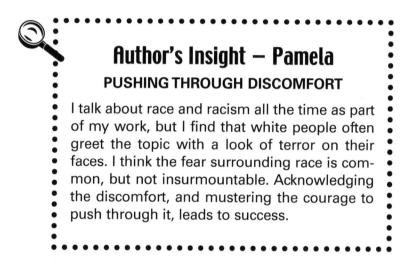

Author's Insight — Pamela
PUSHING THROUGH DISCOMFORT

I talk about race and racism all the time as part of my work, but I find that white people often greet the topic with a look of terror on their faces. I think the fear surrounding race is common, but not insurmountable. Acknowledging the discomfort, and mustering the courage to push through it, leads to success.

UNDERSTAND YOUR OWN CULTURE FIRST

People often want to begin an exploration of diversity by understanding other people's cultures. But they're starting at the wrong place. Understanding another person's culture and world view is only possible if an individual understands his or her own culture and world view first. All aspects of human life are touched by culture, but people often forget that their own thinking and behaviors are culturally based. Without that understanding, they are likely to assume that their own sensibilities are "normal," and that persons who act differently are "strange." This hampers their ability to receive others respectfully and without bias. The anti-racism approach emphasizes that an individual's racial experience profoundly affects the way he or she thinks.

Feelings Are Important

A good conversation about race and racial differences is all about feelings. If you really want to talk about the experience of race, then you must expect that those experiences will bring up emotions. The secret is not to be afraid of the emotions, but to encourage them. Otherwise your conversations will be flat.

Personal Stories Are Powerful

Talking about your personal experiences makes a real difference in changing the racial landscape. When people tell their stories about race, they create powerful connections to others that opinion-sharing alone cannot do.

Change Begins With the Individual

Conversations about race affect individuals. Although racism is a societal problem, there is power in changing individuals because individuals change society. Don't be deterred by the notion that the persons with whom you interact are just a few individuals. As Margaret Mead said, "Never doubt the ability of a small group of committed, thoughtful people to change the world. Indeed, it is the only thing that ever has!"

Learning About Race
Is a Lifelong Process

Don't expect to know everything about race relations and cross-racial communication. Give yourself the opportunity to learn over time. The more you talk with others, the more you learn from your mistakes, the better you get at the conversation, and the better able you will be to make positive change.

Author's Insight – Pamela

THE POWER OF PERSONAL STORIES

While in high school, my son was accused of selling drugs on campus, an offense that would have resulted in his expulsion. He told me that he was in the boys' restroom when a drug deal was being made by two white students. When the students were caught, they told school officials that my son was the one who sold them the drugs. I know my son isn't perfect, but I can tell when he is lying; I knew without a doubt that he was not lying in this matter.

I called the assistant principal who, although she was going to schedule the usual administrative hearing to determine innocence or guilt, let me know that she believed my son was guilty because the other students said so. I felt devastated and angry that my son would come face to face with racism at such a young age. Despite my attempts to shield him, racism had hurt him in one of the ugliest ways possible. He was presumed to be a drug dealer because he was black, and no one believed that other students would make up such a cruel story simply to save themselves.

My own experience with racism told me that I had to take strong and decisive action to interrupt what was happening. My husband and I did our own investigation and discovered that the two students involved in the drug deal were the same two students who, during my son's first days at the school, shouted racial epithets at him, and made comments that they did not "want any niggers at *(cont.)* the school." Using the information my husband and I gathered, the school officials confronted the students, who admitted that my son had nothing to do with the drug deal. They also acknowledged that they agreed to blame him because they calculated that school officials would accept their story because my son was black.

I am deeply affected by the response of other parents to my telling of this story. African American parents often connect to it because they have had similar experiences and relate to the anger and pain that such experiences cause. White parents often connect to the pain and fear involved in trying to protect one's children. The story also helps them better understand racism because they can use their experience of what we have in common—the strong desire to protect our children—to understand how racism feels.

How This Book Is Organized

We have divided *The Anti-Racist Cookbook* into five chapters: PREPARATION, APPETIZERS, SOUPS AND SALADS, MAIN COURSES, and DESSERTS. Generally, we suggest that you work through the chapters in order. Each provides a building block for more weighty discussions that follow. The DESSERTS chapter stands alone, however. Use it anytime you would like to develop personal anti-racist strategies in conversations. Below is a summary of what you will find in each chapter.

Chapter 1: Preparation

Good discussions about race, just like good meals, begin with thorough preparation. Here, we give you the ingredients you need

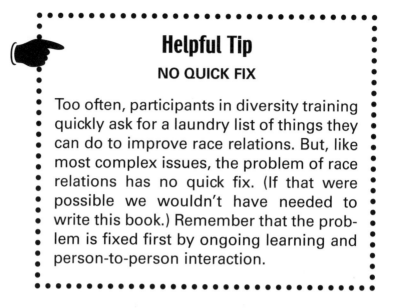

Helpful Tip
NO QUICK FIX

Too often, participants in diversity training quickly ask for a laundry list of things they can do to improve race relations. But, like most complex issues, the problem of race relations has no quick fix. (If that were possible we wouldn't have needed to write this book.) Remember that the problem is fixed first by ongoing learning and person-to-person interaction.

to make your discussions more successful. Included is useful information on goals, group composition and comfort, ground rules, and leading a conversation on race. We also discuss some common pitfalls and errors that you should avoid.

Chapter 2: Appetizers

Just as the first course whets our appetites for the full meal to follow, in this chapter, we give three discussion recipes that will stimulate conversations. The questions are designed to get participants thinking about their cultural backgrounds, the early messages they received about different racial and ethnic groups, and the influences of family, friends, and community.

Chapter 3: Soups and Salads

Once you've done the important work of understanding yourself as a racial person, the Soups and Salads section adds spice to your discussions by focusing on three key areas: (1) the experience of prejudice and discrimination, (2) the experience of racism, and

(3) unanswered questions about racial difference. Working through these discussions will help build bonds of trust and openness with your fellow participants.

Chapter 4: Main Courses

The main course is the heartiest part of a meal, and this final set of conversational recipes includes the three ingredients for addressing the most challenging racial topics. The first discussion addresses whiteness (what it means to be a person who belongs to—or does not belong to—the white race). The second discussion addresses the emotional experience of race in everyday life. The third discussion addresses the commitment participants can make to each other in the future around racial issues. Once you have diligently worked through these discussions, your self-knowledge and ability to relate to persons who are racially different will skyrocket!

Chapter 5: Desserts

Even after the heartiest meal, we can find room for a bit more; therefore, we finish *The Anti-Racist Cookbook* with Desserts, our collection of conversational intervention strategies for the bromides, prejudiced comments, and "politically correct" stock phrases that undermine cross-race relationships. Pull one of these strategies from your pantry whenever you need to.

Chapter 1
PREPARATION

• •

*Success depends upon previous preparation, and without
such preparation there is sure to be failure.*

—Confucius

Preparing for Discussions

Good discussions often feel magical. Everyone is engaged, the
conversation flows freely, the group pays attention to the person
speaking, and disagreements are handled with candor and
respect. Both humor and seriousness are used to improve the
quality of the discussion.

In the following sections, we give you the ingredients that
you can use to make your discussions magical, too. Think of the
discussions as an opportunity to have each participant tell a bit of
his or her story, and you'll have the most success.

Quick Fact

TRADITIONS OF STORYTELLING

Some of the best models for discussions come from the Native American and African traditions of storytelling. In these traditions, there is a strong sense of intimacy between the speaker and the listeners. The art of storytelling is built on the idea that a story takes life only because the speaker shares and the audience listens with great intensity. The speaker is giving of himself or herself, but so too is the audience through the gestures of concentration, attention, and appreciation. Lessen the careful attention to the speaker, show disinterest in the story, and the circuit of intimacy is broken. The speaker no longer takes the audience on a journey with his or her story, and the audience no longer welcomes the speaker as its guide. A sense of community—taking a journey together—is lost.

Setting Realistic Goals

Having conversations about race is usually an exploration into the unknown. Most people think that being well-meaning persons of good will also means that they know most of the answers about racial differences. As a person undertaking a conversation about race, you should set this notion aside. Racial differences are more pronounced than most people realize. The experience of race in the United States, and the way viewpoints are shaped as a result of that experience, is quite different for white people and people of color.

For example, national surveys show that African Americans are less optimistic than white people about the prospects of fair treatment in housing, the workplace, public transportation, and public accommodations. Yet, white people overwhelmingly regard African Americans as being treated *the same* as white people. Likewise, people of color are often surprised to learn that white people do not think of themselves as white people at all (although intellectually they understand that they are white), but instead think of themselves simply as human beings with a loose affiliation to European ethnic groups. Honest conversations about race will bring these different views forward, and highlight the gaps in what people know about the racial experiences of others.

So, as you prepare for a conversation about race, you should have five guiding principles in mind:

1. Use the conversation for learning about others through careful listening.

Listening is the most important ingredient in conversations. Try to listen not only for what others say, but also for the emotions they convey. Give yourself time to reflect on what you hear without prejudgment.

2. Strive to give information about your own racial experience through deep sharing.

Don't wait for others to get the conversation going; share deeply and thoughtfully yourself. Everyone, whether they are a person of color or a white person, has had a racial experience. Share your experience with others, and practice the art of sharing how that experience has made you feel. The best conversations have a strong emotional core.

3. Give yourself permission not to know everything.

As mentioned previously, most people know less about race than they think they do. Relax in the knowledge that you don't have to be an expert on race to engage in a good conversation. Use the conversation as an opportunity to learn about yourself and others. You will probably be surprised about what you don't know.

4. Give yourself permission to make mistakes, and practice the art of doing so gracefully.

If you open yourself to speaking honestly about race, you will probably say things that rub others the wrong way. The greatest learning opportunities arise during these times because you can see how your actions affect others. Avoid focusing on your good intentions—"I didn't mean to hurt your feelings." Instead, practice the art of acknowledging that you have hurt or angered someone, and then express a willingness to understand why.

5. Remember that personal growth happens not only during the conversation, but after the conversation is over.

You'll need time to think about your racial conversations. Use the time between conversation sessions to reflect on your thoughts and the views of others. Personal growth happens not only during the conversation, but during times of quiet reflection.

Makeup of Your Discussion Group

Your racial conversation group should include both white people and people of color. This brings a diversity of racial experience to the discussion. Ideally, there should be more than one person of a particular racial group in your sessions. This lessens the potential of the group to view a single individual as representing everyone in the group to which he or she belongs. Persons who share similar racial experiences are also less likely to feel isolated or put on the spot.

It is advisable to keep the size of your discussion group limited to ten persons or fewer. This will allow you adequate time to have each person participate fully. You can make your groups larger—up to fifteen persons—but you will need to allot more time for each session.

The age of the participants is another important consideration. The discussion guide in *The Anti-Racist Cookbook* is meant for adults. Generally, age sixteen is a suitable minimum. Diversity in age can also add to the discussions. Generational differences and a breadth of life experiences make for greater learning.

As you begin to think about the persons who may be a part of your group, don't forget to consider these individuals:

- Friends
- Family members
- Neighbors
- Coworkers
- Members of your religious organization
- Classmates

Your Discussion Space

It may seem like a small point, but the location and setup of your discussion area make a qualitative difference in how comfortable and attentive your participants will be.

Location and Seating

Choose a room that is large enough for everyone to sit in a circle. This configuration signifies that everyone in the group is an equal participant. Avoid classroom-style seating in which the discussion

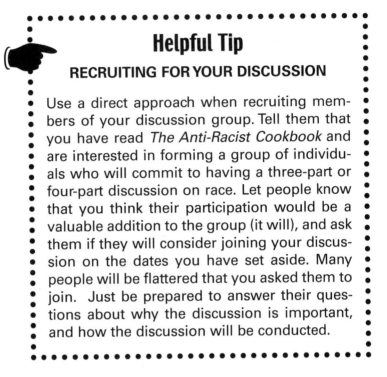

Helpful Tip

RECRUITING FOR YOUR DISCUSSION

Use a direct approach when recruiting members of your discussion group. Tell them that you have read *The Anti-Racist Cookbook* and are interested in forming a group of individuals who will commit to having a three-part or four-part discussion on race. Let people know that you think their participation would be a valuable addition to the group (it will), and ask them if they will consider joining your discussion on the dates you have set aside. Many people will be flattered that you asked them to join. Just be prepared to answer their questions about why the discussion is important, and how the discussion will be conducted.

leader sits at the front of the room—participants will feel as if they are receiving a lecture. A living room, basement area, or meeting room are all ready choices. Ideally, your circle of participants should not have a large boardroom table in the center that gives a sense of formality. Open space in the circle works best.

Lighting

Use bright lighting. Low lighting makes it difficult to read discussion questions and makes some people sleepy.

Temperature

It is sometimes difficult to find a temperature that pleases everyone. If possible, adjust the room temperature to suit yourself, and check

Helpful Tip

SETTING UP YOUR SPACE

If you're using a public space or a space that is controlled by an organization, make sure you speak with the person in charge ahead of time so that he or she knows your needs. Often people assume that classroom-style seating is okay, or that having tables and chairs bolted to the floor will work for every meeting. While you may need to make compromises, we recommend that you do *not* give up sitting in a circle. It sets an invaluable tone. Also, it is a good idea to arrive a few minutes early so that you can arrange the room before the participants arrive.

By all means, use whatever chairs are available, but if you can find comfortable chairs, your participants will be appreciative. Make sure the discussion leader's chair is the same as everyone else's. This will signify equality among the participants.

with the participants from time to time to see if you need to make further adjustments. Ask the participants in advance to wear layered clothing (sweaters, jackets, etc.) so that they can make themselves comfortable.

Privacy

Choose a meeting space in which you will not be interrupted. Turn your telephone off, and by all means ask participants to turn off their cell phones and pagers. Let participants know in advance that you want to have an uninterrupted discussion so they can alert their friends, family, and coworkers not to contact them during your session.

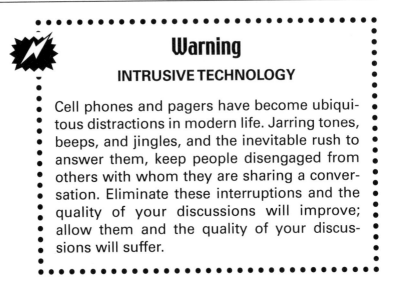

Warning

INTRUSIVE TECHNOLOGY

Cell phones and pagers have become ubiquitous distractions in modern life. Jarring tones, beeps, and jingles, and the inevitable rush to answer them, keep people disengaged from others with whom they are sharing a conversation. Eliminate these interruptions and the quality of your discussions will improve; allow them and the quality of your discussions will suffer.

Refreshments

Light refreshments like coffee, tea, water, and cookies are a nice way to set a welcoming atmosphere. Avoid serving a full meal during a discussion; it causes too much of a distraction.

Allotting Time

Deciding on the Number of Discussions

The Anti-Racist Cookbook is designed so that individuals can use it in three ways: (1) a single discussion of a section, (2) a discussion of a few selected sections, or (3) the discussion of the entire book. Each discussion section will take two to three hours to complete, depending on the size of your group. Whether you are preparing for a single discussion or multiple discussions, facilitator preparation (described in the "Facilitation" section) is always key.

SINGLE DISCUSSION SESSION

Deciding to undertake a single discussion session is okay. If you're just beginning, start with the first discussion set forth in the

Author's Insight – Robin
PREPARING FOR DISCUSSIONS

I always take preparations for discussions with seriousness and delight. For me, setting up a room, preparing coffee, opening windows—all the things necessary for making the room an inviting place—are not only ways to ensure that the participants will be comfortable, but are also ways to prepare myself for leading the conversation. The preparation is like performing a little magic. The room is transformed from an "ordinary" space to a place where something special is about to happen.

Although I know that scientifically speaking the room remains just a room, I also know that changing the room in preparation for a conversation changes the way I think about the room. So, for example, a bland basement setting can become a place where people will share something special and moving. This shift in my thinking helps me be a better discussion leader, and also helps the participants immerse themselves in the dialogue.

As you set up your discussion space, think about the preparation as a series of small rituals. Of course, you will want to observe the basics as outlined in *The Anti-Racist Cookbook*, but also think about adding a twist of your own that makes you feel that the room you are using is now "different." Spraying a favorite air freshener, playing soft music, or even posting a big "Welcome to the Discussion!" note on the wall (flip chart paper works well for that) are all possibilities.

APPETIZERS chapter. A single discussion requires less time in planning, and will often whet the appetite of participants for more. Since you won't have the opportunity to cover "missed" questions during a future session, consider scheduling your session for three hours. Finishing the discussion before time runs out is much better than scrambling to complete the discussion, or ending it abruptly.

MULTIPLE DISCUSSION SESSIONS

Deciding to complete one chapter of this book is a good approach for multiple discussions. The chapters are designed to be used sequentially, so begin with APPETIZERS. When your group completes APPETIZERS, move on to SOUPS AND SALADS, and then MAIN COURSES. Keep the following in mind:

- Many groups decide to meet once per week for two to three hours. This has the advantage of creating a schedule that is predictable, is easy to remember, and doesn't require participants to dedicate several hours for discussion in one day.

- Some groups like to dedicate a longer time for discussion. They may schedule their discussions to meet weekly for a half day or a full day over the course of several weeks. Although it is possible to complete one of the sections in one full day, we advise against this approach. The conversations are weighty, and participants need time to reflect on the experience between discussions.

- If you plan to dedicate more than two hours for any single discussion, make sure that you build breaks into your plan and insert a lunch break if you're going all day.

- Be sure to have your participants commit to attending all of the scheduled sessions. Participant continuity deepens the discussions and adds to the comfort level and feeling of safety within the group.

👉 **Helpful Tip**

GET FULL PARTICIPANT COMMITMENT

Some people will say that they can only attend some of the multiple discussion sessions you plan. Resist the temptation to include them anyway. Instead, tell them that because group continuity is vital, everyone must be available for all scheduled sessions. Tell them that you would be happy to invite them to a future series of discussions.

DISCUSSION OF THE ENTIRE BOOK

Although we believe that the most good comes from discussion of the entire book, planning to do so all at once is probably doomed to fail. The most committed participants will have unexpected work and social obligations that interfere with their ability to attend discussions that are planned over several months. Plan on completing one section at a time over several weeks, then take a two-week or three-week break. Your participants will be more willing to commit to discussing the entire book if they know that they can balance the discussion schedule with the pressures of everyday life.

GUIDELINES FOR USING YOUR DISCUSSION TIME WISELY

To make it more likely that you use your discussion time productively, use the following guidelines:

• Tell participants in advance that you plan to start and end on time.

• Start on time whenever possible. This avoids penalizing participants who are punctual and signals that you take the time constraints seriously.

Author's Insight – Robin
THE IMPORTANCE OF TIMELINESS

I'm at odds with much of the world on the issue of punctuality. I'm a stickler for starting and ending discussions on time—I check my watch constantly. Yet, I know that many people see time commitments as more elastic. They'll arrive a few minutes late, and then the on-time persons must stop to greet them and wait for them to settle in. As a discussion leader, this tends to put me off because my father, an officer in the U.S. Air Force, always impressed upon me the need to arrive on time. Keeping a host waiting was rude, and a sign that we guests didn't have much respect for the preparations the host made for our arrival.

I know that there are a million reasons why people arrive late to their appointments, and many are compelling: an emergency or unexpected travel delay, for example. I also know that for many people tardiness is a habit, even a social philosophy—it's chic to be "fashionably late." Nevertheless, closing the gap between the punctuality-obsessed like me and the habitually late is worthwhile. Starting your sessions at or near the appointed time will:

- allow the participants to use *all* the time set aside for the discussion;
- be fair to the individuals who have arrived on time and who shouldn't be penalized for their punctuality by waiting for latecomers;
- signal that the discussion is not a leisurely social event, but something special that everyone takes seriously.

- End on time whenever possible. Your participants will appreciate your allowing them to attend to other things they have planned, and will think of you as being true to your word.

- Set odd beginning and ending times, such as 2:03 p.m. to 4:03 p.m., for example. Participants will inevitably ask you why you set such odd times, and your answer will be, "...because I'm serious about beginning and ending on time."

- Check the clock periodically.

- Make sure you leave enough time to wind up your discussions with closing remarks.

- Don't try to squeeze too much into a discussion session. If you cannot cover all the questions, let the unanswered ones remain unexplored. It is better to have an in-depth discussion on fewer questions than to move hurriedly just so you can finish all of them.

Facilitation

The discussions in *The Anti-Racist Cookbook* require that one person act as a facilitator for all discussions. The facilitator's responsibility is to ensure that the conversation is as fruitful as possible. He or she ensures that participants adhere to the ground rules the group has established, that everyone has an opportunity to participate in the conversation, that the group uses its time efficiently, and that the group works through any difficulties that may arise. Most important, the facilitator models an attitude of openness and interest in the discussion.

Choosing a Facilitator

People are often reluctant to facilitate small group discussions because they believe that a facilitator must be a professional

Warning
A FACILITATOR IS A MUST

Don't undertake the discussions without a facilitator. If you do, you are likely to find that the conversations will be mostly superficial. Because our society doesn't have good models for racial discussions, people usually resort to unproductive approaches that feel "safe." People will spend their time congratulating each other on not having any prejudices, focusing on the "bad people" (extremist bigots) without examining their own prejudices, defending their points of view about race and racial issues, and offering clichés ("I don't see color." "I treat everyone the same." "We should focus on our sameness, rather than our differences."). A facilitator helps the group avoid these pitfalls.

counselor or social worker who has extensive experience in leading groups. No professional expertise is necessary; however, an effective facilitator has the following characteristics:

- is passionate about the value of conversation;
- is task oriented;
- does not play favorites;
- is open to new ideas;
- does not try to function as the group's expert on race;
- listens carefully;
- watches for nonverbal communication;
- models positive participation;
- is willing to assume the role of facilitator as a primary responsibility;
- is comfortable with the complexity and tension that arise in discussions about race;

- is welcoming of the emotions that arise
  around racial experiences;
- has a commitment to help the conversation succeed.

If you are thinking of becoming a facilitator, think carefully about your ability and willingness to model the characteristics above. It's okay to decide that facilitation is not right for you at present. Perhaps being a participant, instead of a facilitator, is a good place to start. But don't shy away from facilitation simply because you're nervous. Good facilitators always feel a sense of apprehension, especially when they are just beginning. If you've done some self-investigation about racial issues and have the characteristics listed above, then you should consider becoming a facilitator.

If you're not ready to be a facilitator, there is a good chance you know someone who is. As you begin to recruit members of your discussion group, seek out promising individuals. Share *The Anti-Racist Cookbook* with them and ask them to pay careful attention to this section on facilitation. If you let them know that good leadership characteristics—not professional training—are all that are required, a volunteer will step up.

The Small Things That Count a Lot

A recipe is helpful to facilitate any group, but before we get to that, we want to let you know the things that will make you an especially good facilitator, not just an adequate one.

WATCH YOUR ATTITUDE.

Your approach to the discussions means everything to your group, and participants will probably take their lead from you. They will listen not only to what you say, but also to what you communicate through your body language and emotional affect. An attitude of excitement, exploration, and willingness to learn will take you a

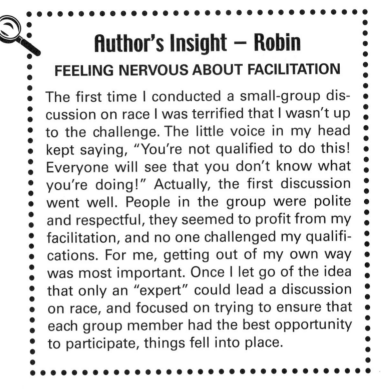

Author's Insight — Robin
FEELING NERVOUS ABOUT FACILITATION

The first time I conducted a small-group discussion on race I was terrified that I wasn't up to the challenge. The little voice in my head kept saying, "You're not qualified to do this! Everyone will see that you don't know what you're doing!" Actually, the first discussion went well. People in the group were polite and respectful, they seemed to profit from my facilitation, and no one challenged my qualifications. For me, getting out of my own way was most important. Once I let go of the idea that only an "expert" could lead a discussion on race, and focused on trying to ensure that each group member had the best opportunity to participate, things fell into place.

long way. Also, a sense of excitement about the wonderful information and stories people share will set a positive tone for your discussion. Be as helpful to your participants as possible. Let them know where the rest rooms are and invite them to have refreshments before the discussion begins. If you treat your participants like honored guests, you will have a greater chance at successful discussions.

SIT IN A CIRCLE.

Always seat participants in a circle. This allows everyone in the group to see everyone else. Eye contact and body language are important forms of communication, which sitting in a circle helps participants observe. Also, sitting in a circle communicates that everyone is equal because there is no one focal person as there is with a classroom-seating arrangement. Make sure that your participants

Helpful Tip
TWO FACILITATORS IS BEST

One facilitator is sufficient, but two facilitators is ideal. If possible, organize your group so that two people (preferably of different racial backgrounds) co-facilitate. New facilitators often feel more confident when they have another person with whom they can share the responsibility for monitoring a group. The different backgrounds of the facilitators also offer wider cultural insights. Having a second facilitator also affords the opportunity to talk about the conversation ("debrief"), and to plan for future improvements when the participants have gone home.

do not sit around a table. Eliminating that barrier sends the message that group members will talk openly with one another.

AVOID NOTE-TAKING.

Ask participants not to take notes during your discussions. Taking notes makes people feel that they are being overly scrutinized and that their confidentiality isn't being respected. Taking notes also keeps the note-taker from being fully involved in the discussion. Instead of listening carefully and watching the nonverbal communication of others, the note-taker is busy with his or her own writing task.

HAVE TISSUES AVAILABLE.

Sometimes your participants will cry. Having a box of tissues readily available means you don't have to stop to find them, and lets the group know that crying is okay, and something you anticipated.

Author's Insight – Pam
CRYING IS OKAY

Although you may feel some discomfort when a participant cries, remember that crying is normal and will sometimes happen in discussions about race. My training as a counselor teaches me that crying is one of the clearest ways that people express what they are feeling; the experience of race can bring up feelings of sadness, pain, and anger. Crying doesn't mean that the participant is in danger or needs to be rescued from his or her feelings. I always tell the participant that his or her tears are welcomed and that there is no need to apologize. I then let the room fall silent for a moment and give the participant time to collect his or her thoughts and to finish speaking. Remember, the more comfortable you are with emotional expression, the more comfortable group members will be expressing their emotions.

Quick Fact
THE TALKING STICK

The talking stick was used in traditional African and Native American cultures as a way to designate who had the right to speak, and to ensure that conversations were orderly and fair. The stick was passed from one person to another until everyone who wished to speak had done so.

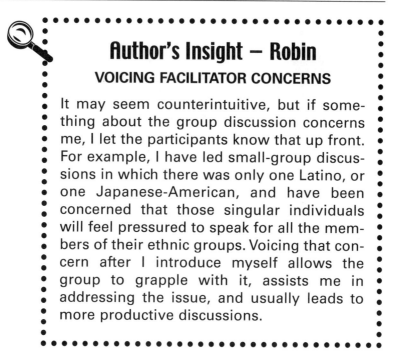

Author's Insight – Robin

VOICING FACILITATOR CONCERNS

It may seem counterintuitive, but if something about the group discussion concerns me, I let the participants know that up front. For example, I have led small-group discussions in which there was only one Latino, or one Japanese-American, and have been concerned that those singular individuals will feel pressured to speak for all the members of their ethnic groups. Voicing that concern after I introduce myself allows the group to grapple with it, assists me in addressing the issue, and usually leads to more productive discussions.

USE A TALKING STICK.

One of the ways to ensure that all participants have a chance to speak fully is by using a "talking stick." Here's how it works. Tell your participants that to keep the conversation orderly and inclusive, the group will use a talking stick to signal who has the group's attention and the go-ahead to speak. The talking stick can be a Koosh Ball, a beanbag, or anything that is lightweight and can be tossed easily from one participant to another. (Remind participants that there is no penalty for bad throwing or catching!) If participants interrupt each other, the facilitator can remind everyone that only the person holding the talking stick has the floor and that others should wait their turns.

DEBRIEF AS YOU GO.

During breaks, take a few minutes away from the group, either by yourself or with your co-facilitator, to assess how the discussion is

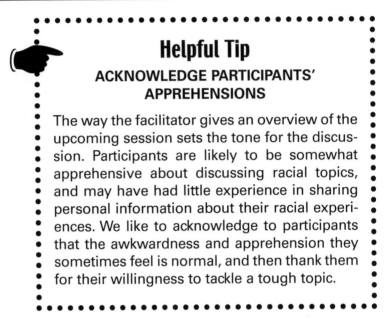

Helpful Tip

ACKNOWLEDGE PARTICIPANTS'
APPREHENSIONS

The way the facilitator gives an overview of the upcoming session sets the tone for the discussion. Participants are likely to be somewhat apprehensive about discussing racial topics, and may have had little experience in sharing personal information about their racial experiences. We like to acknowledge to participants that the awkwardness and apprehension they sometimes feel is normal, and then thank them for their willingness to tackle a tough topic.

going. Think about how the group as a whole is moving forward and how each individual is participating. If you have concerns, think about how you can address them when the group reconvenes. (See the "Cautions and Pitfalls" section at the end of this chapter.)

Recipe for Discussions

INTRODUCTION OF FACILITATOR

As facilitator, you should kick things off because the participants will look to you for leadership. Tell participants your name, the nature of your work, and what drew you to take on the role of facilitator. Also tell participants that you are excited about the upcoming discussion.

OVERVIEW OF DISCUSSION SESSION

Give a brief and general overview of the section of *The Anti-Racist Cookbook* that the group will discuss. Preceding each discussion session is background information that the facilitator can use to introduce that discussion session.

EXPLANATION OF FACILITATOR AND PARTICIPANT ROLES

Explain that the role of the facilitator is to help the group:
- have a conversation that is as fruitful as possible;
- adhere to the ground rules the group has established;
- ensure that everyone is included in the discussion;
- use its time efficiently;
- work through any difficulties that may arise.

Explain that the role of the participant is to:
- listen attentively to the other participants in the group;
- share personal experiences with others;
- be open to the ideas and feelings of other group members;
- help the group stay focused by keeping comments relevant;
- speak freely, but not monopolize the conversation;

Helpful Tip
DEPEND ON ICEBREAKERS

Using an icebreaker as part of the participant introductions goes a long way to help group members relax. In addition to having them share their names and the nature of their work, we usually ask participants to respond to one of these questions:

- What is your favorite food?
- What was your favorite vacation?
- What is something about yourself we can't tell by looking at you?
- What is your favorite thing to do during this season?
- What is your wackiest obsession?

- feel free to disagree with other participants, but do so respectfully;
- discuss but not debate the topic at hand;
- let the facilitator know if help or clarification is needed.

INTRODUCTION OF PARTICIPANTS

Participants need a safe, non-threatening way to begin to talk with one another. Give the participants a chance to introduce themselves by asking them to share their names and the nature of their work.

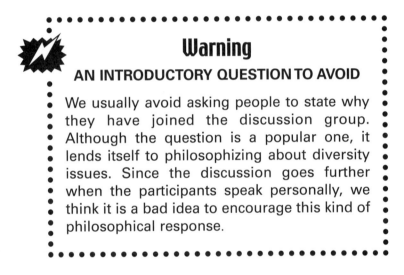

Warning
AN INTRODUCTORY QUESTION TO AVOID

We usually avoid asking people to state why they have joined the discussion group. Although the question is a popular one, it lends itself to philosophizing about diversity issues. Since the discussion goes further when the participants speak personally, we think it is a bad idea to encourage this kind of philosophical response.

SETTING GROUND RULES

Take a few minutes to have the group establish ground rules for its discussion. Ground rules are important because they are guideposts for how the participants will interact with each other. They ensure that the discussion can move forward in a safe and productive environment. They also assist the facilitator in maintaining control over the discussion: reference to the ground rules that participants have established allows the facilitator to correct behavior that is contrary to the goals the group has set for itself.

The facilitator should explain the reason for establishing ground rules. Next, the facilitator should ask group members, "What ground rules should we establish to ensure that our conversation will be open and productive?" As participants volunteer words or phrases for the ground rules, the facilitator should write them on a flip chart or board so that everyone can see them. Allow participants to explain the words or phrases they offer so that everyone understands. The completed list of ground rules should be placed so that everyone can see it during the discussion. If you are meeting more than once, the facilitator should keep the list of ground rules and put it up at the beginning of each session so that the participants are reminded that the ground rules are always applicable.

Below is a list of ground rules that we think are essential for a good discussion. If your group misses some of them, be sure to suggest them yourself.

- Participants will treat each other with respect.
- Everyone will listen attentively.
- Information participants share during the discussion must remain confidential. (Participants are free to talk about the discussion generally, but must not disclose information about other participants without their permission.)
- One person will speak at a time.
- Personal attacks or name-calling are not permitted.
- Participants will strive to speak about their own experience and not generalize or philosophize about "the nature or solution to the issue."
- Participants will refrain from debating issues. (It is okay to disagree, but not to strive to convince other participants they are wrong through a lengthy intellectual discourse.)
- Participation from all participants is encouraged, but participants need not respond to a particular question if they are not ready to speak.

Helpful Tip

THE "OUCH RULE"

Another useful ground rule is the Ouch Rule, which allows the participants to say "ouch" if something said offends them. The Ouch Rule should not be used simply when a participant strongly disagrees with something another participant has said, but only when he or she feels offended or personally attacked. Using the Ouch Rule ensures that an offended participant will not shut down. If your group decides to employ the Ouch Rule, explain that when someone says "ouch," you will suspend the discussion for a moment, ask the offended participant why he or she said "ouch," and then encourage the participants involved to further discuss the issue during a break. It is important that the facilitator not ask the participant who made the "offensive" comment to explain or justify what was said, which would cause the discussion to deteriorate into a debate.

- Participants should not cross-examine one another.
- Participants are encouraged to take risks in sharing personal information about their experiences.
- Note-taking is not allowed.
- Participants will turn off cell phones and pagers unless there is an urgent need to have them on.
- Participants are encouraged to share emotions about personal experiences.

Authors' Insight – Pam & Robin

GROUND RULES TO AVOID

Participants sometimes suggest ground rules that you should not accept:

We should trust each other. Trust is a result, not a rule. Participants can build a sense of trust with one another, but they cannot require trust as a rule to which each must adhere. If participants want to build a sense of trust, they must be open, honest, communicative, respectful, and willing to take risks.

No one should get angry. Anger is a common emotion around race, especially for persons who have been victims of racism. To ask participants not to get angry is to ask them to bury a significant part of their experiences—the opposite of what the discussion is supposed to achieve. Expressing anger about racial issues—or even anger about what another participant says—is okay as long as it does not involve personal attacks, name-calling, or lack of respect for others.

This should not become a therapy session. Of course your discussions will not be psychotherapeutic. That requires a psychiatrist, psychologist, or licensed professional counselor. Establishing a ground rule that your discussions not become a therapy session is therefore like establishing a ground rule that you will not perform open-heart surgery—true, but unnecessary. Often the person suggesting this ground rule is communicating discomfort with the expression of strong feelings. It is best to acknowledge that your discussion is not

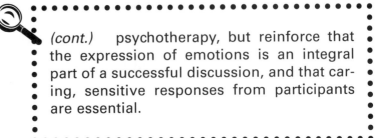

(cont.) psychotherapy, but reinforce that the expression of emotions is an integral part of a successful discussion, and that caring, sensitive responses from participants are essential.

Authors' Insight – Pam & Robin
BODY LANGUAGE SPEAKS VOLUMES

Individuals communicate not only with their words but also with their body language, which has a significant effect on whether participants feel safe, included, and welcomed. We always get a good gauge of how people are feeling not just by what they say, but also by what their bodies tell us. If individuals are sitting with their arms folded or are turned away from others, they are communicating apprehension or discomfort. Individuals who are sitting with an open posture, leaning toward the speaker, and making eye contact are communicating openness and interest. We ask participants to monitor their own body language because it is a strong indicator of their willingness to be receptive to others in the group. We also check in with participants who appear to be uncomfortable by asking them if they are okay.

LEADING THE DISCUSSION AND MONITORING THE GROUP

Begin your discussion by introducing the first question in the section you are using. Use the talking stick to pass permission to speak from participant to participant. When it appears that group members have fully explored a question, ask if participants have anything further to share and, if not, move to the next question. As the discussion progresses, watch carefully to ensure that no one monopolizes the conversation, and that no one is excluded. (See the "Cautions and Pitfalls" section for tips on introverts and extroverts.) After about an hour and a half of discussion, during a natural pause in the conversation, you should give the participants ten to fifteen minutes to take a break. Don't worry about finishing every question in each section. Quality is better than quantity!

CLOSING THE DISCUSSION

Take a few minutes at the end of the allotted time to thank the group members for their participation in the discussion. It is not necessary to restate the content of the discussion. It is important, however, to communicate the value of having an open, honest conversation. If your group will be meeting again, remind participants of the date and time of the next session.

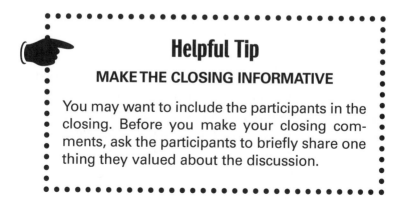

Helpful Tip
MAKE THE CLOSING INFORMATIVE

You may want to include the participants in the closing. Before you make your closing comments, ask the participants to briefly share one thing they valued about the discussion.

Cautions and Pitfalls

Most of us have observed or participated in bad group discussions. They come in various forms: the office meeting in which everyone seems bored and the boss talks too much; the television or radio news program in which the guests scream out their points of view and insult their opponents; or the town forum in which the local politician seems more adept at avoiding the concerns of the constituents than in addressing them.

When discussions go awry they have some common ingredients. Avoid these pitfalls so that your discussions will be fruitful.

THE DISCUSSION BECOMES A DEBATE INSTEAD OF A DIALOGUE.

Debates strive to determine a winning point of view. Dialogues strive to share ideas and an understanding of how the personal background and influences of individuals have shaped perspectives. If a discussion is competitive, the participants are less likely to listen to each other, and more likely to spend their energies trying to dismiss viewpoints they dislike. There is little opportunity for reflection, and because people feel that there are psychological brownie points for discrediting others, insults and personal attacks put participants on the defensive and defeat any chance of learning from each other.

REMEDY: Encourage group members to practice acceptance of what people say about their own experiences and insights. Remind them that the power of discussion is learning not only what opinions participants hold, but also how their experiences have driven them to adopt particular points of view. It is okay to disagree with others, but discussion time is best spent by first acknowledging what others have said to ensure clarity and then offering a different insight from one's own experience. ("Cheryl, I think what I heard you say was....

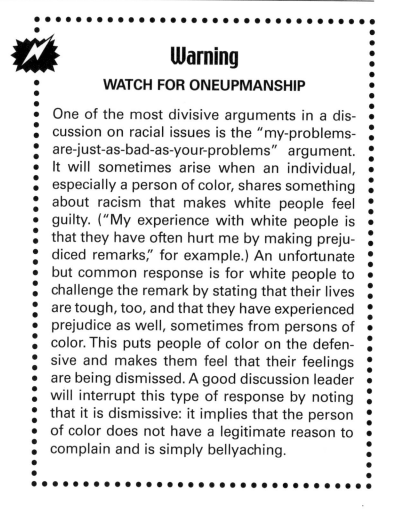

Warning

WATCH FOR ONEUPMANSHIP

One of the most divisive arguments in a discussion on racial issues is the "my-problems-are-just-as-bad-as-your-problems" argument. It will sometimes arise when an individual, especially a person of color, shares something about racism that makes white people feel guilty. ("My experience with white people is that they have often hurt me by making prejudiced remarks," for example.) An unfortunate but common response is for white people to challenge the remark by stating that their lives are tough, too, and that they have experienced prejudice as well, sometimes from persons of color. This puts people of color on the defensive and makes them feel that their feelings are being dismissed. A good discussion leader will interrupt this type of response by noting that it is dismissive: it implies that the person of color does not have a legitimate reason to complain and is simply bellyaching.

My opinion is different on this issue…. These are some of the things that have happened to me that make me feel this way.")

ONE PERSON BECOMES THE "EXPERT" ON THE TOPIC AT HAND.

Experts can be invaluable in many settings. If we need to know something new, a lecture from an individual with special knowledge or expertise will be enriching. But lectures are one-sided.

The audience is there primarily to receive information and the expert is there to impart it. The learning flows only one way— from expert to audience—and the wealth of knowledge from audience members remains untapped. A discussion in which *everyone* is an "expert," i.e., in which all persons are valued because of their willingness to share their experiences and feelings on a topic, will keep the participants engaged, and facilitate learning from the whole group.

REMEDY: If you are the group's discussion leader, don't try to be the expert about race. Remember that your role is to encourage a conversation on race, not to give expert insights or advice. If you find that one of your participants is pontificating too much, you should encourage that person to speak from his or her own experience. ("Bob, your insights are interesting, but I'd like to hear more about your personal experiences on this topic. Would you share some of them?")

EXTROVERTS TALK TOO MUCH; INTROVERTS TALK TOO LITTLE.

Some people are naturally talkative while others feel uncomfortable speaking in a group. But unless this pattern is interrupted, we hear much from the extroverts and little from the introverts. It's not that extroverts don't have anything useful to say and should be silenced, or that introverts should be forced to speak when they choose not to. It's that democracy counts in a group discussion. A good group discussion builds on insights from *everyone*, not just the people who speak most comfortably, articulately, or forcefully.

REMEDY: Ask the group to help ensure that everyone has a chance to participate. If you haven't heard from a group member for a lengthy period, ask if he or she would like to respond. If a participant is monopolizing the conversation, offer appreciation for the participant's input, and then ask the participant to pause for a few minutes so that the group can hear from others. ("John, thanks for offering your thoughts on this. I want to make sure that everyone has an opportunity to be heard, so I wonder if you would pause for a few minutes while we get input from others as well. I want to return to you, however, so that you can add more information.")

PARTICIPANTS BECOME DEFENSIVE.

Conversations about race are challenging because they test the participants' abilities to listen without prejudgment, grapple with their own prejudices, and expose their discomfort about a difficult issue. It is common for participants to consciously or unconsciously try to derail the conversation when emotions or tensions run high. In fact, the participants are becoming fearful of the frankness of the conversation and what it might reveal about themselves, so they become defensive.

REMEDY: Remind the group that strong emotions and discomfort are a normal part of racial conversations, and are healthy as long as participants dedicate themselves to building a sense of community with one another. Occasionally, it is worthwhile to ask group members to sit in silence (perhaps with their eyes closed) for a few minutes of quiet reflection. This allows them time to calm down, and gives participants who might have been silent a chance to offer new insights after a pause.

PARTICIPANTS PHILOSOPHIZE AND
FAIL TO SPEAK PERSONALLY.

"I don't notice whether people are black, white, green, or purple.... We're all the same.... You have to be taught to dislike people because they are different.... Things are better now than they were in the past.... We really should be focusing on the children.... We're preaching to the choir." People feel comfortable spouting these bromides and claptraps instead of sharing information about their experiences, which is more difficult, but more fruitful. Such overworn statements add nothing to discussions about race. In fact, they stifle discussion. People have heard them so often that they become meaningless verbal gestures, and they are mostly untrue. For example, we know that the first thing people notice about others is their gender. The second thing people notice is race. When people say that they don't notice skin color, what they really are trying to say is that they are not prejudiced. That's nice, but doesn't convey anything about their personal experiences around race, which is the focus of the discussion.

REMEDY: Ask participants to speak personally about their experiences, not about their general philosophies on race relations. You may want to say, "We need to be careful about generalizing. Can you talk about your own experience of the question at hand?"

Chapter 2
APPETIZERS

• •

It's important to have a good beginning,
but crucial not to end there.
—The Authors

Talking About Who You Are

Having group members talk about their racial or ethnic origins is the first step in a conversation about race and cultural diversity. You should have the definitions of race and ethnicity, and the terms we use to describe racial and ethnic groups, clearly in mind before you begin.

Definitions of Race and Ethnicity

Race. Race is the classification of persons based on geographical origin and shared physical characteristics like skin color, hair texture, and facial features. Early naturalist Johann Friedrich Blumenbach (1752–1840) categorized humans into five racial groups: Europaeus (Caucasians), the peoples of Europe and the light-skinned peoples of northern Africa; Americanus (Native Americans), the peoples of the Americas; Asiaticus (Asians), the peoples of Asia; Afer (Africans), the dark-skinned peoples of Africa; and Malay (Pacific Islanders), the peoples of Australia and the Pacific islands. As a shorthand, the races were later respectively given the labels, "white," "red," "yellow," "black," and "brown," hopelessly imprecise references to skin color.

Blumenbach and the naturalists who followed him not only classified, but also *ranked* the races. Persons belonging to the white race were on the top of the human hierarchy because they were viewed as the most beautiful and civilized. Persons belonging to the black race were at the bottom of the human hierarchy because they were viewed as having the very opposite characteristics.

Modern science uniformly holds that human racial classifications are invalid. There is no biologically sound way to separate people into racial groups. Even the geographical terminology is wrong. For example, we know that the "white people" of Europe did not originate in the Caucasus Mountains, and hence the term "Caucasian" is a misnomer. All modern humans probably originated in Africa and migrated outward.

Although race is an erroneous *biological* construct for humans, it is nevertheless an important *social* construct. In the U.S., race greatly influences everyday experiences and economic opportunities. The legacy of racial categorization still haunts us today in various forms of racial discrimination and prejudice.

Ethnicity. Ethnicity is the classification of persons based on shared culture, which includes the language, traditions, history, and ancestry people have in common. Ethnicity is not the same as race. For example, Latino/as are an ethnic group, made up of persons whose ancestry is from Central America, South America, Mexico, and certain islands in the Atlantic Ocean. Latino/as may be from different racial groups, however, including white, black, and Native American.

Terms We Use to Describe
Racial and Ethnic Groups

Black. This term was first used by Europeans in the fifteenth century to describe the dark-skinned peoples of Africa, India, Asia, Australia, and the Pacific islands. Later, the European colonists of North America used the term for both Africans and Native Americans and then, over time, for Africans only. "Black" was a shorthand for the relatively darker complexion of Africans, and carried pejorative implications associated with evil and uncleanliness.

Today **African American** is often preferred, but black (either capitalized or not) is still common. The terms *Negro, Colored,* and *Afro-American* are outdated; the first two are considered particularly offensive. Negro derives from the Spanish word *negro,* which means black in color. Colored, once considered a polite name for African Americans (and also Native Americans, Asian Americans, and Mexicans), is viewed as a pejorative allusion to the stereotyped notions of laziness, shiftlessness, and obedience that were attributed to African Americans when the term Colored was in common use after the Civil War and into the twentieth century.

White. As a racial term, *white* now refers to people of primarily European background. Yet, the term is more recent than most people realize. British colonists referred to themselves as "people" or "citizens" or "Christians," not "white people," although others were referred to by their racial categories. In the United States, the term did not always include Jews, the Irish, Eastern Europeans, and Italians, although people in those groups are considered white persons today.

While a European background and relatively lighter skin is usually associated with being white, Asian Indians may consider themselves white despite Asian origins and darker complexion. **Caucasian** is a substitute and popular term for white, but as noted in the discussion on race above, is a geographical misnomer.

Latino/a. The term derives from *latino-americano* and broadly refers to people from Latin America, which includes Mexico, Central America, South America, and those Atlantic and Caribbean islands with Spanish and Portuguese linguistic and cultural origins. It is therefore an ethnic, not a racial term. Although Latin peoples include not only Spanish and Portuguese, but French, Italian, Catalan, and Romanian, those whose languages derived from the Latin spoken by the Romans, Latino/a has a more narrow—Spanish/Portuguese—meaning. The attachment of the trailing "/a" to Latino is a recent addition made to be gender inclusive. (In Spanish, *Latino* refers to men and *Latina* refers to women.) Latino/a is usually not pronounced as written, but as either "Latino" or "Latino and Latina." Latino/a is a term used primarily in the United States.

Persons living in Latin America usually refer to themselves by their ethno-national or ethno-geographic origin (Colombian, Peruvian, Puerto Rican, etc.) The term **Hispanic** is also used in the United States as a substitute for Latino/a, but is losing some ground lately. (As with the term Latino/a, it is not widely used in Latin America.) It is an English language derivation of the Spanish *Hispaña*, the dispersion of Spanish culture into the Americas. In its etymology, Hispanic does not refer to persons with a Portuguese cultural background, but in common usage it includes those persons, too.

Asian/Asian American. These terms refer to persons of southern and eastern Asian origin. The term *Asian American* specifically refers to Asians who live in the United States. Although the continent of Asia encompasses much of Russia and the Middle East, Asian is commonly used as a racial category for persons with origins in China, Japan, and the countries of Southeast Asia. Asian can also refer to persons from the Indian subcontinent, but **Indian American** or **Asian Indian** are often used to refer to persons from the country of India. Other persons from countries on the Indian subcontinent, such as Pakistan, Nepal, Bhutan, and Bangladesh, will refer to themselves according to their country of origin, not as Asian Indian.

Asian is primarily a term used in the United States. Persons living in Asia usually refer to themselves by their ethno-national origin (Chinese, Korean, Japanese, etc.). **Asian and Pacific Islander** (or Asian/Pacific Islander) is an umbrella term that includes not only persons from eastern and southeast Asia, but the Pacific islands as well.

Native American. This term refers to the indigenous people and their descendants living in the U.S. and Canada. **American Indian** or **Indian** is also common, but for many, all three terms are viewed as Eurocentric, either because "America" was the name given by Europeans to the continent, or because "Indian" was the name Columbus gave to the indigenous people he found on his voyage because he thought he had landed in the Indies, the islands of Southeast Asia.

Often, Native Americans prefer to use their tribal names (Siksika) or "nation" names (Blackfeet) rather than the catchall terms above because those terms ignore distinct differences in culture and history. **First Nation People** and **First People**, which came into use in the 1970s, are substitute terms, but are more widely used in Canada. Also note that in Alaska, the term **Alaska Native** is used to refer to the Inuit, Yupik, and Aleut peoples.

Questions for Discussion:

1. What is your racial or ethnic background? Is your racial or ethnic background important to you? Why or why not?

2. What importance did your family place on your racial or ethnic background?

3. What do you know about where your parents and grandparents came from?

4. What do you enjoy most about being a member of your racial group?

5. What do you like least about being a member of your racial group?

Talking About Your Early Messages

Why discuss early messages you received about various groups? Because those messages matter. From childhood we receive messages about the racial and ethnic groups that constitute the world. Some are overt, such as what we learn in school or hear from parents and peers. Others are visual, such as the images we see on television. Still others are hidden, such as the absence of persons from our environment or in our family discussions.

You may have trouble recalling early messages about your own group. These messages are sometimes hard to grasp because you may perceive your own group as just "people." The trick is to think about all the subtle ways that you got the messages that your group was "normal," while other groups were "different." (Consider the racial and ethnic makeup of your neighborhood and school, whether the persons you saw on television looked like you, and who were the people in positions of authority.)

Early messages are powerful because they become deeply ingrained in consciousness and shape our perceptions about ourselves and others. Although early messages are not always negative, they often are bound up in stereotypes. Unearthing those messages is a key step in overcoming prejudices, including prejudices about which we may not be aware.

Warning

THE EARLY MESSAGE TRAP

Because early messages about groups may carry stereotypical themes, you may retreat from sharing them. Fearing possible censure, you may resort to merely voicing your current opinions (probably neutral or favorable) about the groups in question. The result? Empty philosophical speeches designed to convince others that you are not prejudiced. Try to avoid this trap. Early messages are not your current, personal views about the groups listed below, but are the impressions you received as a child or teenager. Recognize that because those early messages came from sources you couldn't control, you are not responsible for their contents.

Early messages about groups are also difficult to share if they are negative and come from family or friends. Who wants to cast the persons they care about in a bad light? But your early messages are not unique: others received the same information. Sharing your early messages is liberating because you give up hiding them as ugly secrets. Early messages are not destiny; they dissolve in the light of open, honest conversation.

Questions for Discussion

1. Share some of your early messages about the groups listed below. As you discuss those messages, also talk about where your messages came from:

Quick Fact

DEFINING STEREOTYPES

Stereotype: Fixed, widely-held images, beliefs, or assumptions about a group of people made without regard to individual differences. Unlike prejudice, which may be formed by a single individual, stereotypes are held by a large number of people in a society. Stereotypes are often impervious to contrary evidence and argument. (Example: Irish people are hot-tempered. Black people are lazy. Jewish people are cheap.)

- Native Americans
- Chinese people
- Japanese people
- Jews
- Arabs
- Mexicans
- Black people
- White people

2. How does your current thinking differ from the early messages you received? Can you recall specific experiences that shaped your thinking?

3. What early messages that you would like to set aside still influence you? What efforts are you making to set those negative messages aside?

Talking About the People Around You

Looking at the people who make up your family, social circles, and work environment can give you further insights about how you form views on race and race relations. After a careful examination of the questions below, you may find that the people of primary influence in your life are not as culturally diverse as you first thought. This offers a challenge to bring "different" people into your world.

Questions for Discussion

1. What is the racial makeup of your immediate family?...of your extended family? Talk about the way race is dealt with in your family.

2. What is the race of your two closest friends?

A. If your friends are of a different race than you, talk about how racial difference has affected your friendship. Do you talk about race? Why or why not?

B. If your friends are of your same race, talk about how racial sameness played a part in the development of the friendship. Are you more comfortable with persons of the same racial background?

3. How racially diverse is your environment (work, school, religious congregation, social circles)? What opportunities do these environments give you to learn about people of racial groups other than your own?

4. If you would like to draw more culturally diverse people into your social and community life, what strategies might you use to do so?

Chapter 3
SOUPS AND SALADS

• •

Honest differences are often a healthy sign of progress.
—Mahatma Gandhi

Talking About Prejudice and Discrimination

The experience of prejudice and discrimination is universal. Everyone has a story in which someone prejudged them and treated them badly just because they were "different." People can be subject to prejudice and discrimination because of their cultural backgrounds, gender, ability, or class, or because they find themselves in situations in which they are viewed as unwelcome outsiders. Sharing experiences of prejudice and discrimination is an important step in building a sense of trust and community.

Questions for Discussion

1. Describe a time when you experienced prejudice or discrimination during childhood or adolescence. How did you feel during the experience? How did you react?

2. Describe a time when you experienced prejudice or discrimination during adulthood. How did you feel during the experience? How did you react? Upon reflection, would you now react differently?

3. How often do you experience prejudice or discrimination in your daily life?

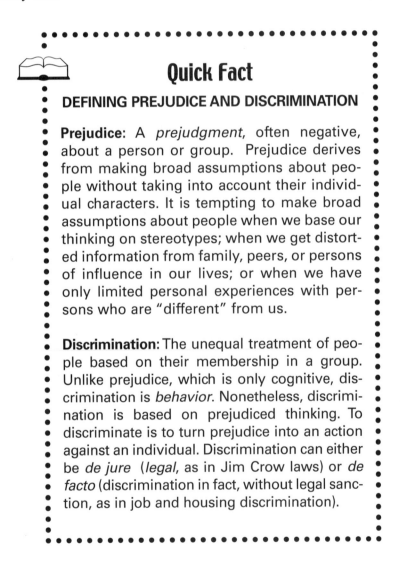

Quick Fact

DEFINING PREJUDICE AND DISCRIMINATION

Prejudice: A *prejudgment*, often negative, about a person or group. Prejudice derives from making broad assumptions about people without taking into account their individual characters. It is tempting to make broad assumptions about people when we base our thinking on stereotypes; when we get distorted information from family, peers, or persons of influence in our lives; or when we have only limited personal experiences with persons who are "different" from us.

Discrimination: The unequal treatment of people based on their membership in a group. Unlike prejudice, which is only cognitive, discrimination is *behavior*. Nonetheless, discrimination is based on prejudiced thinking. To discriminate is to turn prejudice into an action against an individual. Discrimination can either be *de jure* (*legal*, as in Jim Crow laws) or *de facto* (discrimination in fact, without legal sanction, as in job and housing discrimination).

4. What happens when you encounter persons who seem "different" from you because of their cultural background, class, disability, or another factor? Do you ever get nervous, anxious, or fearful? Do you find those situations challenging? Share a time when you have interacted with a person who seemed "different." How did the interaction go? What did you do, and how did you feel?

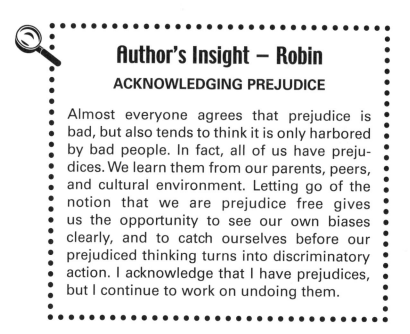

Author's Insight — Robin
ACKNOWLEDGING PREJUDICE

Almost everyone agrees that prejudice is bad, but also tends to think it is only harbored by bad people. In fact, all of us have prejudices. We learn them from our parents, peers, and cultural environment. Letting go of the notion that we are prejudice free gives us the opportunity to see our own biases clearly, and to catch ourselves before our prejudiced thinking turns into discriminatory action. I acknowledge that I have prejudices, but I continue to work on undoing them.

Talking About Racism

The previous section focused on prejudice and discrimination in a general way. This section focuses on racial discrimination and racism. Because both persons of color and white people can have racial prejudices, members of both groups can be targets of racial prejudice and discrimination. Racism, however, is a different matter. We define racism as follows:

RACISM: A society's exercise of racial prejudices against a racial group through that society's institutions of power. Institutional power distinguishes racism from racial prejudice. Institutions such as the courts, schools, legislatures, and businesses have a profound impact on the quality of one's life. When these institutions, supported by the members of the society, create or maintain racially discriminatory practices, remain blind to racial discrimination, or exclude racial groups from the mainstream, they create a societal system of racial oppression called "racism." It is the *collective* impact of racism that makes a difference in an individual's life: racial discrimination acted out by a few individuals is bad, although not always life changing. But racism, racial discrimination acted out by an entire society, erodes the freedoms and degrades the social and economic opportunities for members of the targeted group.

Talking about racism puts us in different camps as persons of color and as white people. Because racism targets the less powerful, in the United States, persons of color find themselves subject to this form of oppression. White people in the U.S., however, are not subject to societal oppression because of their race. (Remember, white people may be subject to racial prejudice and discrimination, but the society as a whole does not act against them because of their race.) But don't let the differences in experiences shut down the potential for learning and building trust.

Acknowledging the differences helps create a genuine sense of community. White people should avoid the trap of rejecting what they hear from persons of color because it seems so foreign. Persons of color should avoid the trap of talking about how they have learned to cope with racism, rather than sharing their experiences and feelings.

Questions for Discussion

1. For persons of color: Share an incident when you have been the victim of racism during your childhood or adolescence. For white people: Share a time when you have witnessed an incident of racism carried out against a person of color who was a child or adolescent.

2. For persons of color: Share an incident when you have been the victim of racism during your adulthood. For white people: Share a time when you have witnessed an incident of racism carried out against a person of color who was an adult.

3. How has racism affected the direction of your life? (For example, if you are a person of color, were you discouraged from pursing courses of study by teachers or guidance counselors because of your race? Or, if you are a white person, did you grow up in a neighborhood that had few or no persons of color?) How might your life be different if you were not affected by racism?

Author's Insight – Pamela
RACISM HURTS EVERYONE

Racism hurts white people too! Because racism promotes stereotypical thinking, it deters white people from forming genuine, close relationships with persons of color. Because racism prevents persons of color from reaching their full potential at work and in the community, it saps the societal brain trust. Because racism is so commonplace, it deadens the sense of moral responsibility and awareness about prejudice and discrimination. Both persons of color and white people have a strong stake in fighting racism.

Talking About Questions
You May Be Afraid to Ask

When children are very young, they ask questions about everything, motivated simply by their desire to know. "Why is your skin brown?" "Why are you in that wheelchair?" "Why do you talk that way?" are all questions that children ask without fear or shame. As children develop into teenagers and adults, however, we send them subtle and overt messages about what is appropriate to ask. Usually such "appropriate" questions are the most empty: "Isn't this some weather we're having?" "How are you?" "Isn't it great that our team won?" Through careful socialization, we've learned to avoid awkward questions which may reveal that we don't understand the racial, ethnic, or cultural backgrounds of others. We've also learned to avoid questions that others might find offensive. This social tap dance leaves us unable to have serious conversations about the ways in which we are different, stifles our ability to learn about others, and keeps stereotypical thinking about others in place.

Having meaningful cross-race conversations means taking a risk to go after information about strangers, and to share information with others about who we really are and who our people are. Getting our burning questions answered gives us a more complete and accurate picture of the people around us. As you enter this discussion, remember that questions about racial differences—especially those involving physical differences for which people have been ridiculed or embarrassed—can bring up painful memories. Also keep in mind that people can only answer questions based on their own racial experience or knowledge. What is true for one individual is not true for every member of that individual's racial group.

Questions for Discussion

1. Have you ever had a question about the physical characteristics of persons of a different race (hair texture, skin color, eye shape, etc.)? What question have you wondered about? *Let other members of the group address your question after you pose it.*

2. Have you ever had a question about the mores, attitudes, and culture of persons of a different race (religious practices, views about affirmative action, foods, language, dress, etc.)? What question have you wondered about? *Let other members of the group address your question after you pose it.*

3. How easy or difficult has it been for you to get information about people of different races? What successes or setbacks have you experienced?

4. How easy or difficult was it for you to pose your questions in this group? How have members of the group supported you as you took the risk to pose difficult questions?

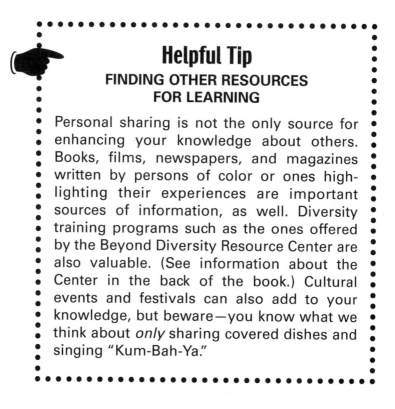

Helpful Tip
FINDING OTHER RESOURCES
FOR LEARNING

Personal sharing is not the only source for enhancing your knowledge about others. Books, films, newspapers, and magazines written by persons of color or ones highlighting their experiences are important sources of information, as well. Diversity training programs such as the ones offered by the Beyond Diversity Resource Center are also valuable. (See information about the Center in the back of the book.) Cultural events and festivals can also add to your knowledge, but beware—you know what we think about *only* sharing covered dishes and singing "Kum-Bah-Ya."

Chapter 4
MAIN COURSES

• •

Where you start is not as important as where you finish.
—Zig Ziglar

Talking About Whiteness

In the United States, the discussion of race usually revolves around the experiences of prejudice and discrimination against people of color. Except in the abstract, white people generally do not see themselves as part of a racial group nor do they recognize that their membership in the white race gives them unique racial experiences. We challenge white participants to begin to understand their experiences as *racial* experiences and not simply *human* experiences.

For example, black people often report that security guards follow them in department stores because they are suspected shoplifters. Being followed because of their race happens so frequently, it is part of the common group experience that black people share. What is often forgotten, however, is that white people have a converse and common experience as well: *never* being followed in stores because of their race. It is easy to think that not being followed because of your race is simply "normal." Actually, it isn't. Many black people (and other persons of color) do not receive such "normal" treatment and must worry about being followed as an everyday occurrence.

The white racial experience of not having to worry about racism shapes the thinking of white people just as the black racial experience of having to worry about racism shapes the thinking of black people. Generally, people understand that racism makes black people angry, tired, and upset, but they have little insight into the ways that *not* having to worry about racism affects white people. The societal advantages of being white, sometimes called racial "privilege," and the way those advantages affect white people are the focus of this section.

The challenge is to keep the white racial experience center stage. This is difficult because the white racial experience is invisible; it is the experience of the majority and is erroneously assumed to be universal. White participants should avoid dismissing the experience of whiteness by assuming that the experience is simply "normal," or by saying that *all* persons should have the privileges that come with being white. Owning the advantages of whiteness, just as persons of color own the experience of racism, will build strong bonds of community within your discussion group.

Before you begin your discussion, think about this list of white racial privileges. Let those experiences inform your discussion of the questions below.

White Racial "Privileges"

- Most skin and hair products are developed for people of my race.
- People of my race do not have to worry about racial profiling by police.

Helpful Tip

INFORMATION ON RACIAL PRIVILEGE

Further help in understanding white racial privilege can be found on the Wellesley Center for Women's website (www.wcwonline.org), where Peggy McIntosh's article, "White Privilege and Male Privilege: A Personal Account of Coming to See Correspondences Through Work in Women's Studies," is available. Also read the articles written by Tim Wise, who is Director of the Association for White Anti-Racist Education (AWARE) at www.zmag.org/bios/homepage.cfm?authorID=96.

- People of my race do not have to teach their children about racism to ensure their safety.
- Positive images of people of my race are widely seen in the media.
- People of my race do not have to overcome negative racial stereotypes.
- People of my race can usually expect to be judged as individuals, and not as part of a "difficult" racial group.
- People of my race can usually live where they please without fear of racial discrimination.
- People of my race can talk with and have lunch with other same-race people and not be perceived as isolating themselves.
- National, state, local, and business leaders are generally people of my race.
- People of my race can talk about racism without being seen as self-seeking, paranoid, or overly sensitive.

Questions for Discussion

1. For White People: What are some of the common experiences of being white? Use the list above to help you focus your thoughts.

2. For White People: What are the advantages of being white in the U.S.? Be sure to think about the ways you *don't* have to worry about race as part of your everyday life—the things you can take for granted.

3. For Everyone: How has the experience of being white, or the experience of not being white, shaped your world view: attitudes and values about family, work, relationships, politics, community, spirituality, etc.?

4. For Everyone: How has being white, or not white, affected your life? Think about how your life would be different if you had to walk in another person's racial shoes.

Talking About the Emotional Journey of Race

Substantive cross-race discussions often shut down because they engender strong emotions. While people of color often feel a sense of pride when they reflect on their racial heritage, they also feel pain and anger when they reflect on their experiences of racism. White people often feel guilty when they hear the experiences of people of color or reflect on their racial advantages. The inability to push through these feelings is what shuts down good cross-race conversations. The ability to talk openly about these feelings helps to keep the conversations going.

As you discuss the questions below, be sure that you push for "feeling" words like happy, sad, anxious, or prideful in your answers. Avoid talking about what you "think," which is your intellectual analysis of a situation. Also be sure to keep your responses personal. Say "I feel," not "You feel," or "They feel."

Questions for Discussion

1. What is your emotional experience around race? What about your racial experience causes you to feel joy, anger, pride, pain, frustration, shame, guilt, a sense of belonging, or a sense of celebration?

2. How have your feelings affected your ability to investigate racial issues or build strong cross-race relationships? Do you feel anxious or comfortable about race...about people from different racial groups?

3. What emotional support do you need from others as you move through your daily racial experience?

Talking About the Commitments We Can Make

Racism can't be solved easily, and certainly not immediately. Working on it is a lifelong process. The questions below allow for a frank discussion of what commitment each individual can make to keep his or her work in anti-racism moving forward. Some discussion groups continue their conversations about race; other groups take on small projects within their communities; still other groups disband, but their members commit to work with each other individually, or work with people in their families, workplaces, and communities.

The questions below are designed to help you think about how you can keep your work in anti-racism moving forward. The final question is one that asks you to share your appreciation for others in your discussion group. Be sure that you are liberal with your praise, and accepting of the praise of others!

Questions for Discussion

1. How willing are you to continue work on race and racial difference? What help will you give to others? What help do you need from others? How will you hold yourself accountable?

2. How do you plan to continue your learning about race and racial differences? What reading, training, and other activities will you undertake?

3. Should we continue our conversations about race with each other in the future? If so, what will be the questions for discussion? How will the conversations be managed (dates, time, place, facilitator)?

4. Tell the members of your group what you appreciate about their contributions to your discussion and their commitment to work on these issues in the future.

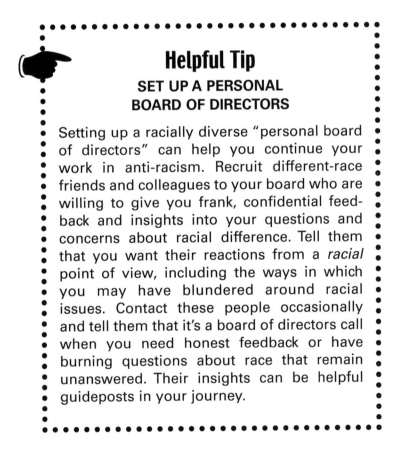

Helpful Tip

SET UP A PERSONAL
BOARD OF DIRECTORS

Setting up a racially diverse "personal board of directors" can help you continue your work in anti-racism. Recruit different-race friends and colleagues to your board who are willing to give you frank, confidential feedback and insights into your questions and concerns about racial difference. Tell them that you want their reactions from a *racial* point of view, including the ways in which you may have blundered around racial issues. Contact these people occasionally and tell them that it's a board of directors call when you need honest feedback or have burning questions about race that remain unanswered. Their insights can be helpful guideposts in your journey.

Chapter 5
DESSERTS

•••••••••••••••••••••••••••••••••••••••

Desserts are an optional part of the meal,
but sometimes the most satisfying.
—The Authors

Conversational Intervention Strategies

It happens all the time: Someone says something mean-spirited, hurtful, or insensitive about a cultural group, or they use dismissive stock phrases to shut down meaningful conversation about race and diversity. Mustering a rejoinder is not always easy. The social or business situation, or the relationship we have with the speaker, can make it awkward, uncomfortable, or even intimidating to respond.

But responding is certainly worthwhile. It is an immediate way that individuals can positively affect the people around them. When we respond to insensitive comments, we raise awareness about diversity and make it more likely that the person with whom we are speaking will be more sensitive when he or she interacts with others.

Don't think that your interventions, though small, will have no significant impact. Even if your responses touch only your family, friends, and coworkers, each of those individuals has connections to many others. The effect of your response can be more far-reaching than you may realize.

People often tell us that they aren't sure how to respond when someone says something that rankles them. Surprise, awkwardness, or the inability to think quickly in the moment makes it hard to formulate an appropriate response. The intervention strategies below give you an advantage: they explain why certain comments need your objection and how you can effectively respond to them.

SOMEONE SAYS, "I DON'T SEE COLOR."

EXPLANATION: Of course, people do see color and race. In fact, studies show that, along with gender, race is one of the first things we notice about others. What people are trying to say is that they don't have racial prejudices and that their "inability" to see color is evidence of that. Working against prejudice, however, is best done by not lying about seeing race in an effort to prove that we are well-meaning. Such honesty avoids the trap of confusing an awareness of an individual's race with a motive to hurt an individual because of his or her racial background. The way to address prejudice and discrimination is to be *conscious* of race. By doing so, we can address racial inequities, and offer empathy to persons whose racial backgrounds are different from our own.

RESPONSE: "I do, but my seeing color doesn't mean I see race as a deficit. Like gender and sexual orientation, race is one of the many factors that defines a person's identity."

Quick Fact
ABOUT COLORBLINDNESS

The idea of a "color-blind" nation first appeared in Justice John Marshall Harlan's famous dissent in *Plessy v. Ferguson*, a case that upheld "separate but equal" accommodations for people of color. Harlan said, "Our constitution is color-blind," and wrote that state laws that mandated "separate but equal" accommodations were unconstitutional. The phrase is often misused to support the notion of a color-blind society in which race does not matter. Actually, Harlan was using the term "color-blind" to say that *in the eye of the law*, white people were not entitled to civil rights superior to those of persons of color. Although Harlan felt that state legislatures could not use "separate-but-equal" statutes to enforce racial inequality, he did not believe that the races were in fact equal. His fuller statement is as follows:

> *The white race deems itself to be the dominant race in this country. And so it is, in prestige, in achievements, in education, in wealth, and in power. So, I doubt not, it will continue to be for all time, if it remains true to its great heritage, and holds fast to the principles of constitutional liberty. But in view of the constitution, in the eye of the law, there is in this country no superior, dominant, ruling class of citizens. There is no caste here. Our constitution is color-blind, and neither knows nor tolerates classes among citizens. In respect of civil rights, all citizens are equal before the law.*

(Cont.) Thus, Harlan opined that people of color were the legal equals of white people; nevertheless, he saw persons of color as socially inferior. We believe that only the former is true, and that, as in Harlan's dissent, advocating color-blindness neither negates underlying racial prejudice nor accepts the notion of racial equality, both legal *and* social.

SOMEONE ASKS, "WHY DO WE NEED TO KEEP TALKING ABOUT RACE?"

EXPLANATION: This often comes up when people feel afraid, overwhelmed, or threatened about racial issues, and they want to stop a useful conversation. Actually, race is not often talked about except superficially.

RESPONSE: "Race is important because we all have one, and our racial backgrounds affect our life experiences in important ways. Our job opportunities, whether or not we are subject to racial discrimination, and how we view society are all shaped by race."

SOMEONE SAYS, "EVERYONE SHOULD PULL THEMSELVES UP BY THEIR OWN BOOTSTRAPS."

EXPLANATION: Most people work very hard; however, few individuals achieve success solely because of their own hard work. Most succeed because they have the additional support of family, friends, community, and social connections. Also, people don't begin their lives with equal advantages. Being reared in a family or community with greater economic wealth or political influence makes success more likely; being reared without those things— one of the usual conditions of being a person of color in the United States—makes success more difficult.

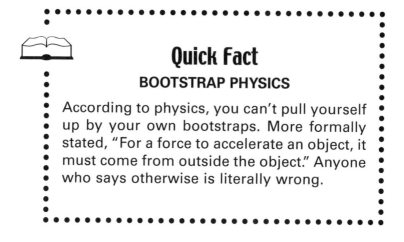

Quick Fact

BOOTSTRAP PHYSICS

According to physics, you can't pull yourself up by your own bootstraps. More formally stated, "For a force to accelerate an object, it must come from outside the object." Anyone who says otherwise is literally wrong.

RESPONSE: "Not everyone has bootstraps to pull and some people don't even have boots."

SOMEONE SAYS, "BLACK PEOPLE ARE RACIST, TOO."

EXPLANATION: Racism and prejudice are not the same. Everyone has prejudices, including black people. Racism, however, is a term that implies the use of institutional power to discriminate against a racial group—something that black people generally cannot do. The comment is often a way to deflect responsibility for making positive change away from the speaker: If black people are racist, so the logic goes, then the speaker doesn't have any responsibility to work on his or her own prejudices.

RESPONSE: "Black people, like everyone else, have prejudices, but that doesn't minimize the work that white people need to do to address racism."

SOMEONE SAYS, "BUT SLAVERY HAPPENED A LONG TIME AGO...IT'S NOT MY FAULT."

EXPLANATION: The effects of historical events reach way into the future and have long-lasting ramifications. The ramifications of slavery affect the social, economic, and political opportunities of African Americans in the United States. African American college graduates earn about 20 percent less than their white counterparts. It wasn't until the 1960s that larger numbers of African Americans were permitted to attend colleges and universities to help improve their economic futures. A thorough study of U.S. history must link past events to current experience. Yet when it comes to slavery, people often balk at making that connection. Although talking about slavery may be painful or embarrassing, ignoring slavery keeps people from understanding its consequences in the present day.

RESPONSE: "It isn't your fault, but it is your responsibility to address what the legacy of slavery continues to do to African Americans and our society as a whole."

SOMEONE SAYS, "I'M NOT PREJUDICED."

EXPLANATION: We don't give anyone brownie points for claiming not to have prejudices; everyone has them. The real trick is having a dedication to working against them. This requires giving up the pretense of being an unprejudiced person and getting in touch with your own prejudices, many of which will be unconscious. Often the phrase, "I'm not prejudiced," is followed by the qualifier "but" with a justification for the very prejudice that is disclaimed.

RESPONSE: "I think everyone has prejudices, including me. Given the societal messages about race and racial difference, it's impossible not to. Acknowledging personal prejudices is a first step to undoing them."

SOMEONE SAYS, "SOME OF MY BEST FRIENDS ARE BLACK."

EXPLANATION: Just because an individual has friends of a different race doesn't mean the individual is free of racial prejudice or that he or she has nothing to learn about handling racial issues in a respectful manner.

RESPONSE: "That's great, but let's talk about the issue at hand."

SOMEONE SAYS, "LET ME TELL YOU A JOKE ABOUT THE BLACK MAN, THE CHINESE MAN, AND THE PARROT...."

EXPLANATION: Racial and ethnic jokes perpetuate stereotypes and are harmful—even if members of the "targeted" group are not present. Because the jokes are meant to be funny and people often say they "don't mean anything by them," the jokes are a sneaky way to put people down and reinforce negative thinking about cultural groups. The ramifications are enormous. Listeners get the message that "those people" are fodder for ridicule, and although it wouldn't be "politically correct" to make overtly disparaging comments about them, they can be humiliated because it is "just a joke." Even if the speaker is a member of the joke's targeted group, telling racial or ethnic jokes is no less harmful. It still castigates the targeted group and promotes stereotypical thinking.

RESPONSE: "I'd really rather not hear that kind of joke," or "Please don't tell that kind of joke around me," with an explanation of why it is bothersome.

SOMEONE SAYS, "HE DIDN'T MEAN ANYTHING BY THAT; HE'S JUST JOKING AROUND."

EXPLANATION: This comment usually arises when someone is trying to excuse a racist comment made by a third party. Humor is not an excuse for insensitive comments, however, because humor is one of the primary ways stereotypes are perpetuated. The key here is to put the defending party on notice that the behavior is inexcusable and that the issue should not be dismissed.

RESPONSE: "He may not have intended the comment to be offensive, but it was to me."

SOMEONE ASKS, "AREN'T THINGS BETTER TODAY?"

EXPLANATION: Although there have been significant strides made in civil rights, the plight of persons of color remains economically and socially difficult. Often when people ask this question, they are suggesting that there is no social justice work left to do. In fact, a careful examination of income statistics, incarceration rates, and discrimination patterns in education, housing, and employment shows that racial inequities still exist.

RESPONSE: "Things have gotten better, but there is still significant work to be done. The playing field still isn't level."

Author's Insight – Robin
SOCIETAL PROGRESS ON RACE

My great grandfather was a slave. My grandfather lived in rural poverty. My father graduated from college and later earned a doctoral degree. I'm an attorney and have lived in the middle class all my life. Things have gotten better for me, my family, and many persons of color. But what makes the United States great is not how we celebrate our progress, but how we push ourselves to meet our stated values and ideals, and grapple with our shortcomings.

SOMEONE SAYS, "I'VE BEEN THE VICTIM OF PREJUDICE, TOO."

EXPLANATION: This comment usually arises when an individual wants to minimize the experience of persons of color by making it the same as or less painful than their own experience. Of course white people experience prejudice, but it is divisive to diminish the experience of racism by playing the "I've-been-hurt-too" game.

RESPONSE: "Since you've been the victim of prejudice, you can use that experience to begin to understand how racism feels. Understanding racism is important because it hurts persons of color all the time; we need to talk about racism so we can combat it."

SOMEONE ASKS, "ISN'T THAT REVERSE RACISM?"

EXPLANATION: There is a difference between being hurt by prejudice and discrimination, and being oppressed by racism. Prejudice and discrimination are carried out by individuals; racism is carried out by institutions (courts, schools, businesses, etc.) that reflect the dominant culture, which in the U.S. is the culture of white people of European descent. Reverse racism is a misnomer because it presumes that racism is the same as prejudice and discrimination. This comment is a way to say that "black people are prejudiced too," or that black people are asking for "special privileges" through programs such as affirmative action.

RESPONSE: "Black people have prejudices like everyone else, but racism is an institutional problem that hurts persons of color. Let's talk about issues of fairness and keep issues of institutional power and historical discrimination in mind."

SOMEONE SAYS, "JUST TELL ME WHAT I HAVE TO DO."

EXPLANATION: White people sometimes expect a list of quick (and easy) things they can do to eliminate racism. We wish that there were such a list! Unfortunately, eliminating racism is not like implementing a new math curriculum. Racism is a long-existing problem that our society has been struggling with since its inception. It will take multiple approaches and hard work to solve.

RESPONSE: "Dedicate yourself to a lifelong pursuit of the elimination of racism. This work begins with your own education about racial identity and racism, and includes striving to eliminate racism in your own environment."

SOMEONE SAYS, "YOU'RE PREACHING TO THE CHOIR."

EXPLANATION: This comment usually comes from individuals who believe that they understand all they need to know about racism, and that further conversation or learning needs to be focused on "those other people." Learning about anti-racism, however, requires a commitment to lifelong learning and the willingness to be a perpetual student as well as a teacher.

RESPONSE: "Even the choir members need to listen to and learn from the sermon."

SOMEONE SAYS, "YOU (A PERSON OF COLOR) HAVE TO TEACH ME (A WHITE PERSON) WHAT TO DO TO ADDRESS THIS PROBLEM."

EXPLANATION: White people sometimes believe that the only way that they can learn about racism is from people of color. In fact, people of color tire of teaching about racism because what they say is frequently rejected. Other sources of knowledge about racism include books, movies, magazines, newspapers, documentaries, and training workshops.

RESPONSE: "I'll help you if I can, but let me share information about the other resources that are available to you."

SOMEONE SAYS, "MAYBE IF WE JUST TALKED ABOUT HOW WE'RE ALL THE SAME, WE WOULDN'T HAVE THESE PROBLEMS."

EXPLANATION: Talking about how we are the same is easy. Talking about how we are different is not. Although we *are* more the same than we are different, it is our differences that keep us isolated from each other. A willingness to have challenging conversations about cultural differences builds true respect and trust.

RESPONSE: "Even though it's difficult, talking about how we are different will help us better understand each other's experiences. Otherwise our conversations will remain superficial and unproductive."

SOMEONE SAYS, "ALL THIS DIVERSITY STUFF IS TOO COMPLICATED FOR ME."

EXPLANATION: This statement often comes from individuals who are daunted by the ambiguity that comes from the discussion of cultural issues or are frightened of or resentful about change. "How am I supposed to know whether to call someone 'Black,' or 'African American,' or 'Latino,' or 'Hispanic?'" is a typical refrain. In fact, understanding diversity is complicated—but it is also achievable. An acceptance of ambiguity and individual differences is necessary for sorting out the complexities.

RESPONSE: "It is complicated, but keep at it."

SOMEONE SAYS, "I TREAT EVERYONE THE SAME."

EXPLANATION: People who make this statement usually mean that they try not to treat people unfairly based on race. But, this is not a one-size-fits-all world: we think, act, and feel differently based on all our experiences, including those that are cultural and racial. Unconscious prejudices still work against persons of color in jobs, housing, and social situations. In addition, treating everybody the same implies that we should ignore cultural differences. That minimizes the experiences of persons of color because they receive disparate racial treatment all the time.

RESPONSE: "I think that what you're really saying is that you try not to treat people badly because of their race. Treating people badly should be avoided, but treating people differently—but equitably—based on their cultural backgrounds may be necessary if you want to treat them with true respect."

SOMEONE SAYS, "YOU'RE JUST TOO SENSITIVE ABOUT RACIAL ISSUES."

EXPLANATION: This statement is usually directed at people of color, who are more aware of racial issues because such issues affect their lives with regularity and intensity.

RESPONSE: "Perhaps you're not sensitive enough about racial issues. We need to talk about why we have such differences in perception."

SOMEONE ASKS, "WHY ARE BLACK PEOPLE ALWAYS SO ANGRY?"

EXPLANATION: When black people talk about race, they often express feelings of anger associated with racism. Rather than retreating from the anger, white people should understand that anger is a natural response to unfair treatment. Using their own experiences of times when they have been angered because of mistreatment will go a long way to help them empathize with black people.

RESPONSE: "Like all people, black people become angry when they are treated badly. Try to recall what feelings of mistreatment have felt like in your own life. That may help you understand."

SOMEONE SAYS, "I'M ONLY ONE PERSON; THERE'S NOT MUCH I CAN DO."

EXPLANATION: Addressing racism can seem overwhelming, and there are times when it seems that the efforts of one individual are futile. But individuals striving for change make great differences in the lives of the people around them. Anti-racism work helps heal the effects of racism on those who are its victims. Although being an active anti-racist may feel lonely, you don't have to work alone. Forming alliances with groups and individuals can give you support in continuing your work.

RESPONSE: "One person can make a difference. You can make a difference in the lives of the people around you. Don't get discouraged."

SOMEONE SAYS, "WE SHOULD REALLY WORK ON THE CHILDREN. THEY ARE OUR FUTURE."

EXPLANATION: This comment is particularly irritating because it comes in the guise of extending help to young people—something that most people would never argue against. Helping young people is a necessary step in fighting racism. Nonetheless, this statement implies that children should be the sole targets of diversity work, and that adult work is unnecessary or hopeless. In fact, good work with children on anti-racism requires that the adults who teach them have done their own homework first.

RESPONSE: "As adults, let's do our own work first. Then we'll be better prepared to work with children."

SOMEONE SAYS, "I DON'T CARE IF PEOPLE ARE BLACK, WHITE, PURPLE, OR GREEN."

EXPLANATION: As far as we know, there are no purple, green, or polka dot people. This comment trivializes racial differences. It is an adoption of colorblindness in its worse sense because it doesn't take into account how racial differences drive personal experiences and institutional oppression. It also implies that conversations about racial and cultural differences are not worthwhile because, at the heart of things, everyone is the same. Although everyone does have universal "human" experiences, too often colorblindness is a demand for persons of color to put aside their cultural and racial experiences.

RESPONSE: "Race matters in the U.S., and we shouldn't trivialize its importance by comparing it to fictional persons who have skin colors that don't exist in nature."

Parting Comments of Hope

● ●

Many small people, in many small places, doing many small things can change the face of the world.
—Quotation from the Berlin Wall

So, we have had a wonderful, satisfying meal together. Everyone is full and has enjoyed one another's company, but we must now part.

We hope that you will remember this meal always, and invite guests to share similar meals with you over and over again. The more we engage in "real" conversation, the more we learn and grow.

Remember that although the number of guests at your table may be small, we have great hope for change. After all, the effects of a ripple on a pond can be far-reaching.

Resource List

• •

Here are some resources that we have found valuable as we have worked to deepen our understanding of cultural differences. We recommend them to you.

BOOKS

Arabs in America: Building a New Future by Michael W. Suleiman

Asian American Dreams: The Emergence of an American People by Helen Zia

Asian American Panethnicity: Bridging Institutions and Identities by Yen Le Espiritu

Bury My Heart at Wounded Knee: An Indian History of the American West by Dee Alexander Brown

Changing Race: Latinos, the Census and the History of Ethnicity in the United States by Clara E. Rodriguez

Civility: Manners, Morals, and the Etiquette of Democracy by Stephen L. Carter

Color-Blind: Seeing Beyond Race in a Race-Obsessed World by Ellis Cose

The Color Complex: The Politics of Skin Color Among African Americans by Kathy Russell, Midge Wilson, Ronald Hall

Dismantling Racism: The Continuing Challenge to White America by Joseph Barndt

Face to Face: The Changing State of Racism Across America by James Waller

Faces of the Islands: When Pacific Islander and American Ways Meet by Willard C. Muller

Harvest of Empire: A History of Latinos in America by Juan Gonzalez

Latino Manifesto: A Critique of the Race Debate in the U.S. Latino Community by Bridget Fenner and Christopher Rodriguez

Lifting the White Veil: An Exploration of White American Culture in a Multiracial Context by Jeff Hitchcock

Margins and Mainstreams: Asians in American History and Culture by Gary Y. Okihiro

Native American Testimony: A Chronicle of Indian-White Relations from Prophecy to the Present, 1492–2000 by Peter Nabokov

The Nature of Prejudice by Gordon W. Allport

The New Face of Asian Pacific America: Numbers, Diversity, and Change in the 21st Century by Eric Lai and Dennis Arguelles

1001 Things Everyone Should Know About African American History by Jeffrey C. Stewart

Pedagogy of the Oppressed by Paulo Freire

Race: How Blacks & Whites Think & Feel About the American Obsession by Studs Terkel

A Race Is a Nice Thing to Have: A Guide to Being a White Person or Understanding the White Persons in Your Life by Janet E. Helms, Ph.D.

Race Manners: Navigating the Minefield Between Black and White Americans by Bruce A. Jacobs

Race Matters by Cornel West

Racial Healing: Confronting the Fear Between Blacks & Whites by Harlon L. Dalton

Showing My Color: Impolite Essays on Race and Identity by Clarence Page

Uprooting Racism: How White People Can Work for Racial Justice by Paul Kivel

When Race Becomes Real: Black and White Writers Confront Their Personal Histories by Bernestine Singley

"Why Are All The Black Kids Sitting Together in the Cafeteria?": And Other Conversations About Race by Beverly Daniel Tatum, Ph.D.

ARTICLES

Collection of Articles by Tim Wise on Anti-Racism, www.zmag.org/bios/homepage.cfm?authorID=96

"Detour-Spotting for White Anti-Racists" by Joan Olsson (cultural bridges), HC81 Box 7015, Questa, NM 87556 USA

"Social Change or Status Quo? Approaches to Diversity Training" by Patti DeRosa (ChangeWorks Consulting, Randolph MA), changeworksconsulting.org

"White Privilege and Male Privilege: A Personal Account of Coming to See Correspondences Through Work in Women's Studies" by Peggy McIntosh (Wellesley Center for Women), www.wcwonline.org/seed/unpacking.html

VIDEOS

The Color of Fear (Stir-Fry Productions), www.stirfryseminars.com

The Essential Blue-Eyed (with Jane Elliott), California Newsreel, www.newsreel.org

Ethnic Notions: Black People in White Minds (California Newsreel), www.newsreel.org

Index

lighting (*See* discussion space: lighting)

listening, 27

m

Malay, 58
McIntosh, Peggy, 77
Mead, Margaret, 20
messages, trouble recalling early, 62

n

Native American, 61
Negro, 59
note-taking, 41

o

Ouch Rule (*See* ground rules: Ouch Rule)

P

participant(s)
 age, 29
 defensiveness, 52–53, 55
 diversity, 28
 number, 29
 people to consider, 29
 philosophizing, 46, 55–56
 recruiting, 29
personal board of directors, 80
philosophizing (*See* participant(s): philosophizing)

Plessy v. Ferguson, 83
political correctness, 13
"preaching to the choir," 90
prejudice(s)
 defined, 68
 origins and proliferation, 68
privacy (*See* discussion space: privacy)
privilege(s), white racial
 further reading on, 77
 list, 76–77
punctuality (*See* time management: importance)

R

race
 biological construct, 58
 classifications, 57–58
 defined, 57–58
 economic consequences, 11
 national survey findings, 27
 social construct, 58
race riot, Los Angeles, 12
racism
 anger about, 49, 92
 defined, 69–70
 distinguished from racial prejudice, 69
 hurting people of color and white people alike, 71
 sensitivity about, 92
 teaching about, 90
red, shorthand for racial category, 58

About the Authors

Robin Parker is a diversity consultant who has built a national reputation for innovative work on anti-racism issues. His training efforts have focused on building more inclusive communities, schools, and workplaces through diversity education. Before joining the Beyond Diversity Resource Center as Executive Director, Parker served as a Deputy Attorney General in the New Jersey Division of Criminal Justice, and Chief of the Office of Bias Crime and Community Relations.

Parker received his Juris Doctor degree from the University of Illinois Law School, and bachelor's degree in English from Rutgers University. He is the recipient of numerous awards, including the World of Difference Award from the Anti-Defamation League of the B'nai B'rith, the Rachel Davis Dubois Human Relations Award from the International Institute, and a Merit Citation from Stockton State College's Center on Hate Crime and Extremism.

Pamela Smith Chambers is a leading specialist on race and cultural diversity issues. She has a commitment to help people confront institutional racism and oppression through personal growth and change. Before joining the Beyond Diversity Resource Center as Training Director, Chambers was the Supervising Program Development Specialist in the New Jersey Office of Bias Crime and Community Relations and, prior to that, the Director of Counseling and Education Services at the YWCA of Trenton.

Chambers received an M.S. in Counseling and B.A. in English, with a minor in African American Studies, from Trenton State College. She also serves as an adjunct faculty member at Mercer County Community College, where she teaches English.

About the Beyond Diversity Resource Center

The **Beyond Diversity Resource Center** is a nonprofit organization that works to build a society that sincerely honors individuals because of their cultural differences. The Center advances the moral imperative of respect and dignity for all persons through diversity education and training.

Diversity

The Center's diversity training helps participants explore issues of oppression, prejudice, bias, and stereotypes in their own lives and in the lives of others. Participants are challenged to examine how racism and other forms of oppression damage individuals and society. The training prepares individuals to participate in the creation of a respectful, multicultural society that honors the background and experience of all individuals.

Community Dialogue

The Center's work in community dialogue brings together diverse individuals to talk about issues such as diversity, violence, education, or police-community relations. The discussions are small, informal conversations led by skilled facilitators. Exploding the myth that talk is not action, community dialogue enhances trust among participants and promotes cooperation on issues of common interest.

Organizational Development

The Center's work in organizational development provides ongoing consultation, education, and training necessary for an organization to change its institutional environment and create a climate that is inclusive. The Center joins with businesses, school districts, and city, county, and state governments to foster this cultural transformation.

Organizational development strategies include partnering with clients to raise individual and group awareness, and reshape institutional policies. This unique work focuses on systemic change aimed at achieving fairness and equity within organizations while enhancing productivity.

We would like to hear from you!

If you would like more information about the Beyond Diversity Resource Center's programs or would like to receive a brochure of classes, please call (856) 235-2664, or visit the Center's website at www.beyonddiversity.org.

 Beyond Diversity Resource Center

Notes

Notes

Notes

Notes

Notes

Notes

Notes

Notes

Notes

Notes

Notes

Notes

Notes

Notes

Notes

Notes

The Anti-Racist Cookbook

Order Here
or Check Your Leading Bookstore

❏ **YES**, I want _____ copies of *The Anti-Racist Cookbook* at $14.95 each, plus $3.00 each for shipping and handling. (New Jersey residents add $0.90 sales tax per book.) Canadian orders must be accompanied by a postal money order in U.S. funds. Allow 15 days for delivery.

❏ **YES**, I am interested in having Robin Parker and Pamela Smith Chambers speak or give a seminar to my company, association, school, or organization. Please send information.

My check or money order for $_____ is enclosed.

Please charge my ❏ Visa ❏ MasterCard ❏ Am. Express ❏ Discover

Name _____

Organization _____

Address _____

City/State/Zip _____

Phone _____ Email _____

Card # _____

Exp. Date _____ Signature _____

Please make your check payable and return to:
Crandall, Dostie & Douglass Books, Inc.
245 West 4th Avenue • Roselle, NJ 07203

Call your credit card order to: (908) 241-5439
or Fax: 908-245-4972